Blood Makes the Grass Grow

MIKE PESHMERGANOR

M000080519

MIKE PESHMERGANOR

Copyright © 2018 Mike Peshmerganor

Cover design by 556 Productions

Translated by Bjarte Abildsnes

Edited by Katherine Row

All rights reserved.

ISBN: 9781718059177

BLOOD MAKES THE GRASS GROW

For Susanne. Thank you for putting up with me. I would have been lost without you.

MIKE PESHMERGANOR

CONTENTS

MIKE PESHMERGANOR

ACKNOWLEDGMENTS

This book could not have been translated to English without generous financial aid from the following: Joosep Aasamets, Alex Aiken, Byron Alvarez, Barry B., Ronan Cogley, Timothy Neville Cormier, Daniel Delgado, Matthew Florez, Erik Grassauer, Gunfighters Only LLC, Court Hill, Bill Johnson, Kevin Kee, Michael S. King, Ben Langille, Jere Leppäluoto, Kevin Lewis, Juan Camilo Londono, Marko Loubser, Jonathan "Battery" M., Steve Madsen, Michael Marburg, Lukas Martinez, Michael J. Miller II, Thomas Murawsky, Bret Newbould, Tyler Nobbley of Cave Creek, Robert Onsøien, Keith Poyser, Pål Røkholt, Irving Rosenstein, Edward Schaefer, John Sherrick, Roger Shulze, Garrett Smith, Aleksander Telepov, Tom, Rory Tonkin, Marcus Torgerson, Trey, Johan Uyttersprot, Reid Weigum and Daniel Zamora.

From the bottom of my heart, thank you.

I am also forever grateful to my editor, Katherine Row, who volunteered months of her time, tactical knowledge and linguistic expertise to the English edition.

MIKE PESHMERGANOR

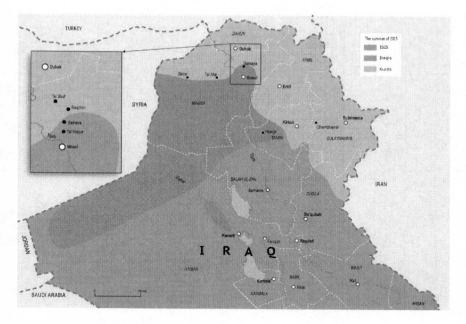

MAP OF IRAQ, THE SUMMER OF 2015.

MIKE PESHMERGANOR

PROLOGUE

Northern Iraq, May 3, 2016

ISIS is burning oil. The heavy, black smoke is meant to hinder Coalition aircraft's line of sight. The neighboring town, beyond the frontline, belongs to the caliphate, ISIS, or "Daesh" in local parlance.

I've been at the front for more than a year and, of course, the enemy had to launch its major offensive just when our commander has taken his first leave in years. General Wahed Kovle, a former hitman, has served jail time for murder. But for the last few years he has stuck to fighting ISIS terrorists, becoming one of the most feared, respected and legendary leaders in the Kurdish Peshmerga forces. The general is a man I would follow to Hell and back; but he's in Beirut now.

Intense gunfire erupts on our right flank. Through the dense smoke, I can't see what our neighboring unit is shooting at.

"What's happening, boys?" I ask our guys on the front line.

"Daesh is attacking our neighboring troops," one replies.

I move halfway up the berm and turn my scope towards the shooting, unable to see anything through the acrid smoke. Hirani, a Kurdish comrade from Sweden, throws himself down in the closest machine gun position. After two weeks in the unit, he still hasn't been issued a firearm and must rely on the squad's weapons.

My hunting instinct is turned on. I tell Hirani to settle in and ready his machine gun, then I run toward the gunfire, stopping several times to appraise the situation.

"Hey, how's it going?" I ask as I leap into another machine gun position, spraying dirt and sand over the two young soldiers inside. Their response is interrupted by a massive explosion followed by an enormous cloud of smoke where the battle rages.

11

"They're attacking with suicide vehicles," one replies.

"Watch your sector and stay low," I say and take off running. I'm high on adrenaline. There's no greater rush than war. Just a few hours earlier I brashly told Hirani that ISIS wasn't capable of executing a full-scale attack at our front. Now it seems they are.

A handful of guys man our last position. I find a spot among them and scan our right flank. We're about 450 yards from our neighboring unit's nearest position. I can see activity and it's tempting to run over to them. Haji, one of our officers, is apparently a mind reader.

"Stay here, Mike. No matter what happens, we're not to leave our area of responsibility," he reminds me.

Another suicide vehicle explodes. Through my scope I see a wave of enemy vehicles approaching our flank. One, two, three, four.... I count ten to twelve cars coming towards us.

"Haji!" I shout. "What the fuck is going on?" Unless Daesh has laid a bridge across the trench, they can't get those vehicles across the frontline. Does ISIS have their own pioneer troops who can lay bridges?

"Grenade!" a voice shouts.

A mortar grenade strikes just over a hundred yards behind us. I barely have time to throw myself down before shrapnel hits an empty oil barrel next to me, making a sharp "ping" as it penetrates the steel. A yellow puff of smoke rises from the ground.

"What's that, chemicals?" Haji asks.

Although I'd never experienced a chemical attack before, I've read enough to realize these grenades are filled with chlorine gas. More grenades lands around us, some dangerously close. The effect of the gas is limited. I'm more worried about shrapnel. I stay as low as possible, observing the enemy through my scope. Three ISIS vehicles approach our frontline.

The neighboring unit responds with a wire-guided anti-tank missile. The missile's operator can lead it to the target after it's fired, even one that's moving. Eagerly I follow the missile's path to the three vehicles. From my vantage point, everything moves in slow motion. In reality, the missile travels up to 220 yards a second.

"It missed on all three," I tell Haji, disappointed, as the missile passes the third vehicle and detonates harmlessly. Germany has supplied the Peshmerga with an arsenal of wire-guided missiles. They probably should have spent more time training the operators.

Our neighboring unit's machine guns ring sharply, then several of their vehicles fully loaded with retreating soldiers drive towards us at full speed. One of our guys, Karwan, stops the traffic and asks where they are headed.

"Daesh has broken through the front. It's hopeless," a fleeing soldier says with panic in his voice. "We have to get away from here and reorganize." I look toward the flank. A seemingly endless row of enemy vehicles is headed toward us.

"Shame on you!" Karwan shouts. "How can you leave now?"

A growing flood of cars and trucks filled with fleeing soldiers and heavy weapons rolls past our position. A neighboring officer urges us to join them.

"Do you see over there? Do you see Daesh crossing the frontline with armored vehicles and hundreds of soldiers?" he says. "They laid a bridge over the trench. We have nothing to stand up to them with, and neither have you."

Damn, how I miss the general. He would have shot this deserter on the spot. Again, they urge us to flee with them.

"So, there's no one manning the closest position?" Karwan asks in disbelief. The officer shakes his head.

"We have abandoned all our positions." Rage builds inside me. They've left our right flank completely open.

"Then I'll man it myself!" I shout and start running. After all, "Peshmerga" means "those who face death."

1 THE BEGINNING

It began with a news report. The Islamic State, or ISIS, had been heavily featured in the media throughout the summer of 2014. The terrorist group had conquered several Iraqi cities and towns, among them Mosul, one of the country's largest municipalities. ISIS seemed unstoppable as it stormed one Iraqi city after another, driving the government forces before them.

I had followed the Syrian civil war with great interest since its outbreak in 2011. I knew ISIS had originated in Iraq in 1999, and that during the civil war it had grown into one of the largest and most feared jihadist groups in Syria.

Toward the end of June 2014, ISIS circumvented Islamic tradition and illegitimately declared itself a caliphate. The terrorist group broadcast a propaganda video shot on the border of Syria and Iraq featuring Bastian Alexis Vasquez, a Norwegian-Chilean foreign fighter from the town of Skien. Vasquez proudly showed off several cowering prisoners and an Iraqi border station taken by ISIS.

The terrorist group's progress puzzled me, and I was deeply disturbed that so many Europeans, including Norwegians, had joined it. What if these foreign fighters returned home? As part of an increasingly racialized Islamist movement and with fresh combat experience from Syria and Iraq, these recruits could pose a great threat to the West.

It was August 2014. Summer vacation was over, and I was back at Camp Rena in Norway where I worked as a soldier in the elite Telemark Battalion. Over the last few days the situation in Iraq had worsened dramatically. Until then, ISIS had not directly attacked the Kurds or the Peshmerga, the Kurdish forces in Northern Iraq, but had concentrated their offensives

15

against Iraqi forces in the rest of the country. During the first two weeks of August, ISIS had conquered vast areas of Northern Iraq, including the Kurdish town of Sinjar. It was a news report from Sinjar I saw.

I watched images of Yazidis, a religious minority ISIS considered "devil worshippers," burying their dead children on the Sinjar Mountains. I heard stories of ISIS forcing non-Muslims to convert to Islam; of thousands of men dumped in mass graves; of women taken to Mosul and Tal Afar and sold in the markets as sex slaves.

Walking back to the barracks after a workout at the gym I met Dilshad, a Kurdish friend who worked in one of Telemark Battalion's combat support companies. He was livid.

"Have you seen what's happening in Kurdistan?" he said. "Those fucking cocksuckers took Sinjar and are slaughtering the inhabitants! They're killing everyone, and no one does anything!

"I'm considering going down there; just quit my job and go help. I can barely sleep, thinking about what those poor people are going through. They're raping women and children!"

I hadn't been to Northern Iraq since my family fled in the '80s when I was an infant. I barely spoke the language and didn't know the culture as well as I perhaps should. I'd never envisioned returning so I never bothered to learn the heritage. I had always felt more Norwegian than Kurd, but the Islamists' ravages in the Kurdish areas woke something in me. Nevertheless, I wanted to stay professional and keep a cool head.

"Wait a bit, Dilshad," I counselled. "The Americans are bombing now, and you shouldn't ignore the possibility of Western boots on the ground soon. Maybe we'll be involved in some way then. That's better than going down on our own."

We went our separate ways, and I urged him again not to make a hasty decision. I fervently hoped the international community would intervene soon.

By mid-August, several Western nations had committed to contribute militarily to halting ISIS' advancement in Iraq. They also agreed to help local authorities handle the humanitarian disaster which, among other things, involved more than a million people displaced in their own country.

The US took the lead and formally requested Norwegian troops. Then-sitting Prime Minister Erna Solberg categorically rejected the request. Norway would, however, send a C-130 Hercules transport aircraft to carry humanitarian aid to Iraq. One Hercules against ISIS? How half-hearted was that response?

By then, the UN Security Council had alluded to ISIS' genocide against the Yazidis in Northern Iraq. So why didn't we do more? Had we forgotten the lessons from Rwanda and Bosnia, where no one intervened until it was too late?

Norway's Hercules aircraft made a single trip to Northern Iraq in September before returning for good to Gardermoen military airport. As it turned out, the aircraft had never been needed. The mission had been purely symbolic on the Norwegian government's part.

In September, the war against ISIS was high on the agenda of a NATO summit in Wales. I paid close attention. Maybe the Norwegian government would step up to the plate after all. But no, the prime minister stuck to her previous response.

I couldn't believe it. What was the point of having a military dimensioned for international operations if it wasn't used? I could think of no better reason for Norway to send troops abroad than to stop ongoing genocide.

And what about all the Europeans who had joined ISIS? Didn't we have a responsibility to stop our own citizens from perpetrating war crimes and other atrocities in Iraq? Who would prevent them from returning home and carrying out terrorist attacks in our own cities? I realized it was futile to wait for Norway to engage directly in the war against ISIS. I would have to act on my own.

Mankind's history is one of violence; peace is an anomaly. Children born in Northern Iraq in the mid '80s learned this early. Iraq and Iran were at war and Kurds in Northern Iraq, who long had suffered under the Iraqi regime, sided with Iran under what was to become one of the deadliest conflicts since the Second World War.

In 1988, in retaliation for Kurdish support of Iran, Iraqi dictator Saddam Hussein vowed to eradicate the Kurds. In the short but deadly Anfal campaign, the Iraqi regime massacred more than 180,000 civilians in Northern Iraq. Most were Kurds, but other groups perceived as disloyal to the regime were also slaughtered.

My parents are Kurdish, and my father had been politically active, not the best combination at the time. Shortly after I was born, my family fled to Iran. They resorted to using human traffickers, who lead us across the mountainous border on horseback. The smugglers' contraband, be it humans, weapons or other goods, was an attractive target for Iraqi aircraft, and during our escape the refugees behind us were bombed. No one survived. Our group escaped only because we found cover in a grove shortly before the attack.

My mother and I narrowly missed plunging down a mountain from a path carved into a cliff that was just wide enough for a horse. The blanket she carried me in unfastened and her shriek as I slid free panicked the horse, which almost careened down the steep mountainside.

I don't remember my time as a refugee, but I've been told I loved the bombs' loud thuds and powerful flashes of light we witnessed during our escape, like a little child experiencing fireworks for the very first time.

We were placed in an overcrowded camp in Iran. Although Iraqi Kurds originally supported Iran in the war, our allegiance was not reciprocated. Among other atrocities, my big brothers and I were forced to watch a Kurdish teenage boy getting brutally whipped for having a relationship with a local girl. I cried throughout the ordeal.

We lived in this refugee camp for a year and half before we managed to move to Syria. After three months in the capital, Damascus, we traveled to Europe and finally to Norway.

My earliest childhood memories are from the reception center in the small Norwegian town of Fagernes. I remember local teenagers revving their moped engines in the evening. I remember getting chocolate eggs for Easter. And I remember the small plastic toy soldiers my big brothers and I played with. The soldiers came with us when we moved to a small place outside the town of Hamar. They occupied me for hours.

As I got older I graduated to action figures. They were larger than the toy soldiers, with moving joints and more details. I was fascinated by their boots, the different patterns and colors of the camouflage uniforms, the cartridge belts across their muscular torsos and, of course, their weapons. I was sold. A soldier was what I wanted to be.

I didn't play much with other children in the neighborhood. I wasn't interested in ball games, football cards or pedal cars. I preferred sitting in our basement den watching my big brothers' VHS movies when they were away. Where other children idolized Eric Cantona and Michael Jordan, my heroes were Arnold Schwarzenegger, Sylvester Stallone and Chuck Norris. I wanted to be like the silent, strong heroes from my favorite movies.

Reality, though, was quite different. I had been seriously ill during the journey to Europe and remained underweight throughout childhood. I never had an appetite and was malnourished as a result. In addition, I was riddled with anxiety and nightmares and was often scared and insecure without obvious reasons. I suffered a constant, general feeling that the world was a scary and dangerous place. There were many trips to the school nurse and the child psychologist. Skinny and scared, I didn't have much in common with John Rambo.

Nevertheless, my interest in the military never really faded. In the mid '90s, my brothers served their mandatory military conscription at the garrison of Porsanger. I was proud when they came home on leave in their uniforms and told me about boot camp and the survival exercises. I could barely wait 'til I was old enough to serve.

A few years later, I got a taste of what the Norwegian armed forces offered during my school's work week at Camp Terningmoen in Elverum. It was a big deal for a 15-year-old kid to dress up in a uniform, march around a field, and shoot a G3 rifle and MP5 submachine gun, weapons I knew well from video games. Young and ignorant as I was, I felt ready for my conscription and continued service in the military.

Now I just had to finish school, which I hated more than anything else. Whether it was a lack of motivation or learning disabilities I don't know. This was before ADHD was commonly recognized, so I was never tested for this or any other learning disorders.

History was the only subject I enjoyed. In math class, I secretly read about ancient Greek history or medieval Europe. I quickly understood that fighting was human nature. To kill the enemy, take their women and children as slaves, and burn their homes had shaped civilizations throughout the millennia. This was how it had always been and always would be. It was a grim realization but thinking anything else was naive. I believed I should prepare for a coming war so I could protect myself, my loved ones and my values.

After two years of high school I'd had enough. I got my big brother to drive me to the conscription center in Hamar at Ridehuset, a late 1880's depot that had been converted to the armed forces administrative offices. With determined steps I walked through the black wrought iron gate to the old parade ground. I went from building to building trying all the doors until I found one unlocked. Inside, an officer sat in the office closest to the entrance. I knocked on the open door.

"What can I help you with, young man?" he asked in a forthcoming manner.

I explained that although I was due to start my conscription in a year, I wished to begin earlier since I was done with school. The officer offered me two options, border ranger at the garrison of South-Varanger, or His Majesty the King's Guard. I was familiar with the King's Guard but had never heard of the border rangers. Since border ranger service started a couple of months before the King's Guard I chose that. I was eager to get started. That night I sat at my computer and researched. The border rangers seemed like an exciting service and I looked forward to traveling north, blissfully ignorant of the reality that awaited me.

On a frigid night in January 2004, a C-130 Hercules transport aircraft carrying us new recruits landed at Camp Høybuktmoen in Kirkenes. I sat in the back of the plane where cold air whipped in from the cargo ramp. I was frozen stiff before we arrived.

Insecurity seized me as I stepped from the plane into the icy wind and biting cold. I was a nerd who had spent most of his teens in front of a computer screen at home or with other nerds at computer gatherings; a slender, untrained youth who had barely been in the wild before. Suddenly it struck me that maybe I wasn't prepared for what lay ahead.

As fresh recruits, we were placed in the Training Company. Those who passed the six-month program would transfer to the Border Company and spend the last six months of their conscription as rangers on the Norwegian-Russian border. Those unfit to serve at the border would be assigned to the Garrison Company as camp guards, drivers or kitchen assistants. Garrison rangers didn't exactly have the same status as those on the border.

During boot camp we spent a lot of time out in the cold. Our packs were heavy and we travelled long distances on skis. Everything we did was exhausting and I struggled like a dog in the snow. During ski marches I frequently fell, buried in the deep drifts under my seventy- to ninety-pound backpack, to the great annoyance of my fellow recruits who helped me up. To say I was not fit to be a border ranger is an understatement.

After the first field exercise I volunteered for the Garrison Company, hoping for an easy position as a guard. My application was rejected. Unhappily, my platoon leader saw some potential and ordered me to continue in the Training Company. The truth probably was that many of my fellow recruits also applied for easier Garrison Company service. While I wasn't special forces material, I apparently wasn't the worst.

After half a year of mediocre motivation and wavering effort in the Training Company I was finally a border ranger. During boot camp, I had abandoned my plan to continue in the armed forces beyond conscription, but receiving the black and yellow cord on my uniform was a proud moment nonetheless.

Now I was tasked with monitoring and patrolling the Russian border. Real missions with live ammunition boosted my enthusiasm. What I had earlier learned made sense now. In small teams with little interference from officers, we manned observation posts for several hours every day and did long patrols along the border in all kinds of weather over steep, difficult terrain, both on foot and on snowshoes. Slowly, my physical strength and stamina improved, and I became more robust and confident.

Winter arrived as my conscription neared its end and I decided to continue in the military. I had progressed a lot during the last year and thought a few more years in the armed forces would turn me into a man. Of course, I also hoped for deployments abroad.

A year and a half earlier, an American-led coalition had invaded Iraq and

toppled
Saddam Hussein's regime. Norwegian forces were on the ground in Iraq and Afghanistan, but their role had been relatively innocuous. There was never any talk of Norwegian soldiers engaging in combat, apart from the Norwegian Special Forces who hunted Al-Qaeda and Taliban leadership in the Afghan mountains. Nevertheless, traveling to a conflict zone and experiencing what life could offer beyond safe Norway seemed exciting. I sent an application to the elite Telemark Battalion.

The Telemark Battalion was founded in 1993 as a light infantry battalion of conscripted soldiers garrisoned at Camp Heistadmoen in Kongsberg. In 2002, the Battalion was moved to Camp Rena in Hedmark County and reorganized into a mechanized infantry battalion comprised solely of professional soldiers and officers. If you wanted deployments abroad, this was your unit.

In the spring of 2005 I got a rejection letter citing the large number of applicants. My mood plummeted, but I decided not to dwell on it. I moved away from home and got a job in Oslo with genial colleagues and a good salary. Half a year later I bought a brand-new apartment outside Oslo. Life was pretty good, but something was missing. I had some potential I couldn't unleash in civilian life. My dream of becoming a soldier wasn't entirely dead.

2 AFGHANISTAN

One morning before work, I found an enticing brochure for the Norwegian Home Guard's Task Force in my mailbox. The newly established Task Force consisted of select soldiers who were better trained and equipped than the regular Home Guard. The Task Force of each districts' Home Guard would form the tip of a spear that could mobilize rapidly to defend national security. Because my conscription was relevant, I had been chosen to apply. It was just part-time, but the idea of being a soldier in what seemed like a professional unit was alluring.

In the fall of 2008, I travelled to Camp Lutvann in Oslo to apply to Task Force Derby in the Home Guard district of Oslo and Akershus. The other candidates and I received a briefing about Derby service and completed the initial selection, followed by physical tests and an interview, which I got through fine.

We were outfitted in uniforms and transported to Camp Heistadmoen for the main selection over the weekend. Selection was surprisingly hard, with long marches at high pace, grappling and shooting with little food or sleep. I travelled home late Sunday evening exhausted, bruised and scratched but elated. I had a sense of achievement. A week later I was offered, and accepted, a position in Derby.

Throughout 2009 I took part in numerous exercises and courses in addition to my civilian job. Many skilled soldiers and officers served in Derby, but enough time elapsed between exercises that I didn't get the improvement I craved. I was no warrior yet.

That December I received an email from my squad leader. Derby was sending a team to Afghanistan for a six-month deployment in July 2010. Was I interested? Without thinking twice, I volunteered. In the new year I would undergo a short assessment at Camp Huseby in Oslo, where eight lucky soldiers would be selected for deployment. I completed physical tests and an interview and was overjoyed when I received the phone call I had been waiting for. I was going to Afghanistan!

The Derby team would be embedded with the Norwegian National Support Element, or NSE, whose main base was Camp Marmal outside Mazar-i-Sharif. NSE was tasked with providing logistical support for Norwegian forces in Afghanistan including transporting supplies and other cargo between Norwegian camps in convoys of military trucks with mounted MG3 or .50 caliber machine guns. Most NSE positions were advertised on the Internet and anyone could apply, even civilians with no military experience.

Until then, the convoys had travelled on their own. But as security worsened in Northern Afghanistan, where most Norwegian soldiers were stationed, the convoys felt exposed. The new team would support the convoys with force protection. The force protection team sought eight soldiers with relatively similar military backgrounds. For that reason, the mission was given to Derby.

From January to April, I trained with seven strangers under some of the best instructors from our district's Home Guard, including several from the Home Guard's special HV-016 unit, which was disbanded later that year under great controversy. Behind that decision stood then-Chief of Defense Harald Sunde, who reportedly had his own motives for the shutdown.

My teammates seemed very professional and committed, but with a fair share of humor among them. We clicked as a team and got to know each other well. Our team would be distributed on two force protection vehicles, four men per vehicle. I was assigned top cover to man the mounted .50 caliber machine gun on my vehicle's roof. I also had to master other weapons, including an MG3 machine gun and an 84mm recoilless rifle.

With many resources available, our team quickly met expectations. I shot several thousand rounds with the MG3 machine gun, based on the German MG42 from World War Two. I loved the high rate of fire, the recoil hitting my shoulder and the smell of gunpowder. It was an instant favorite. I daydreamed about wielding this weapon against the Taliban, not because I hated the enemy, although I despised their ideology and their actions, but because the more we trained, the greater my wish to see combat. I wanted to be tested, and war was the ultimate trial.

In April we travelled to Bardufoss in Northern Norway for the three-month pre-deployment phase. We would get to know the other NSE soldiers and train together until deployment. The first two weeks were an endless stream of PowerPoint presentations and lectures about Afghanistan. I quickly realized that warrior culture and combat skills weren't this unit's focus. My team made the most of it, and after three months of training, we were finally ready to mount missions in Afghanistan.

Before deployment, we were given a week's leave to spend with family and friends. I was home alone when I got a text message from Ronny, chief of the force protection team.

"Four Norwegian soldiers killed by a roadside bomb in Afghanistan," was all it said. I couldn't believe it. I switched on the TV2 news channel. The alert at the bottom of the screen confirmed the tragedy. Norway had been involved in the war in Afghanistan since 2001, and until 2010 only four Norwegian soldiers had died in combat, very few compared to our allies. But in January 2010, a soldier from the Telemark Battalion was killed when his infantry fighting vehicle hit a roadside bomb. And now four Norwegian soldiers had been killed in a single incident.

With this news, it got harder to convince my parents that the mission was as safe as I'd described it. My mother cried. My father tried to persuade me not to go, with no luck. I was fully aware of the dangers and risks, but my wish to take action, to experience combat, had only grown stronger. It was a risk worth taking.

I looked forward to leaving. My team was convinced we would see action during the next six months and I spent a lot of time visualizing the engagements. Would I stay calm and act as I had been trained? Or would I become paralyzed or panic? Would I lose control of my bladder and gut, a physiological reaction many soldiers experience during battle? Would my bullets hit their mark? How would I feel afterwards? I looked forward to getting the answers to my many questions.

In July, we finally arrived at Camp Marmal outside Mazar-i-Sharif. Dry air and intense heat engulfed us as we stepped out of the plane. At almost 120 degrees Fahrenheit in the shade, it didn't take long for sweat to start pouring.

The camp was enormous and housed several thousand Allied soldiers from many nations, mostly the US and Germany. We were bussed from the airport to the Norwegian section, Camp Nidaros, where NSE was stationed. It would be our home for the next six months. Here cargo and goods were flown in from Norway and transported to other Norwegian camps and field bases around Afghanistan. In addition to escorting convoys, my team would regularly fly to the capital, Kabul, to function as military escorts during important visits from Norway.

After establishing ourselves at camp, my team prepared for our first mission, escorting a supply convoy from Camp Nidaros to the Norwegian Camp Meymaneh in Faryab Province.

My driver, Richard, thoroughly inspected our vehicle to ensure everything was in order. He refilled oil and fluids and cleaned the bulletproof windows. Thomas, my team leader, checked our communications, GPS and maps. My battle buddy Magne and I mounted the .50 caliber machine gun on the roof and loaded in the other weapons, ammunition, water and energy drinks. We would secure the rear of the convoy, while the other force protection vehicle drove in front. We were excited about the potential to see some action, but the seven-hour drive to Meymaneh was uneventful.

"Maybe something will happen on the way back," Magne said hopefully, as we stretched our legs and roamed the camp while the supplies were being unloaded.

The stabilization force stationed in Meymaneh, known as Provincial Reconstruction Team Meymaneh, or PRT Meymaneh, was the largest Norwegian force in Afghanistan. It had a small infantry unit comprised mainly of soldiers from the Telemark Battalion. We had heard a lot about them in Norway as they saw a lot of action and often engaged in offensive operations. These were the big boys. We looked up to them, and it was exciting to see what vehicles, gear and weapons they used on the battlefield hunting the enemy.

Magne had been top cover on the road to Meymaneh, so it was my turn to man the .50 caliber machine gun on the return trip. I loaded the gun and covered my face with a scarf as the convoy headed out the main gate. I had a HK416 rifle, a 40mm grenade launcher and several grenades under the hatch. I felt ready and hoped someone would be stupid enough to engage us. But the trip back was without incident, which became the template for most of our missions.

Although we operated in high-risk areas we were never directly attacked. Sure, the job of force protection and military escort was defensive in nature, but with all the combat Norwegian forces were seeing during that period, I still hoped to experience some myself. Many of my team members felt the same.

Before every mission, Magne and I hyped ourselves up, saying this was the mission where we would finally see combat. Not because we believed it, but because that mindset ensured we were mentally sharp and more meticulously prepared for the mission. If we were confronted by the enemy, weapons and other equipment must be ready.

Magne got sick shortly before our last mission in January 2011. Thomas, Richard and I dropped by the hospital tent to find him lying alone on a field bed reading a magazine.

"Oh well, Magne, last mission now," Richard said jokingly. "Too bad you'll miss the action." Magne's mood turned sour.

"Okay, I'm happy for you if you experience combat. But if you come back and boast about it, you're assholes." We laughed even harder and left to prepare for the mission.

I thought about the conversation. Magne would be sincerely happy for us if we saw combat, if we were shot at, with all the risk that involves. Not because he wished us harm but because he loved us and knew we craved action. Was there something wrong with us? I silently acknowledged that this is how any soldier feels who has trained for war over an extended period. This was our new normal.

We weren't comfortable discussing our feelings outside the force protection team. Warrior mentality as such was not really accepted in the NSE. Leadership seemed more focused on welfare and social events, planning volleyball tournaments, movie nights, waffle frying and even a theater play. Did they think we were in Christian camp?

Leadership had cancelled several of our missions, citing security concerns, even though other countries were operating in the areas we were avoiding. On one occasion, Norwegian forces, including the supply convoys, were detained in Camp Marmal for two weeks following a rumor of a possible suicide bomber on a moped in Mazar-i-Sharif. German helicopters were hired to transport supplies to the Norwegian camps. I would like to see that bill.

Although there were skilled and good individuals in NSE, I lost further respect for the organization after an Allied soldier was killed in action. We were to pay our last respects at a procession in his honor at Camp Marmal before his final flight home. My mind drifted as we lined the road on which his coffin would be transported to the awaiting aircraft. Who was he? How had his last minutes been? Did he suffer, or did he die quickly? Who was waiting for him back home?

As the truck carrying the fallen soldier neared our stretch of the road I heard giggling to my right. I looked over to see a message being whispered from ear to ear. Judging from the reactions, a joke was being passed around the Norwegian contingent. The man next to me got the whisper and leaned into my ear with a smile.

What's for dinner? Pass it on," he whispered. I stared in disbelief.

"Are you kidding me?" I demanded. His smile vanished, and he excused himself saying he had just been passing the message along. I was deeply embarrassed for our country. This would never have happened in PRT Meymaneh. There they showed respect for fallen brothers in arms, no matter their nation. There they had warrior culture.

The truck passed slowly, and we saluted the coffin.

In January 2011, after half a year in Afghanistan, we landed at Gardermoen military airport for a stopover before going home. For many soldiers returning from operations abroad, the shift from life in the field to life back home can be drastic and emotional. To ease that transition, the

Norwegian armed forces arranges a three-day stopover, usually at a nice hotel in a big city abroad, where soldiers talk to a psychologist, evaluate the deployment and enjoy nice dinners and the chance to socialize with their units.

Our stopover, however, was at a hotel in rural Gardermoen. On the third day we returned to the military airport for a medal ceremony with family and friends attending. Then-Minister of Defense Grete Faremo and Chief of Defense Harald Sunde were also present. It was a visit I could have done without.

A few months earlier, the newly launched men's magazine Alfa had published a story on Norwegian forces in Afghanistan that caused a media uproar in Norway. The editor and a photographer had spent a week in Afghanistan and, among other things, had ridden in my vehicle during an operation.

The editor seemed shady at the time. It was obvious he was only after headlines to promote the launch of his magazine. He had baited us with leading questions, but my team had been suspicious and kept our mouths shut. Unfortunately, he had also spent a few days with the PRT Meymaneh infantry unit. The headline "War is Better Than Sex" in big letters in the magazine's first edition was a Telemark Battalion soldier'taken completely out of context.

In a clear attempt to save their own skins, Faremo and Sunde addressed the media before the story got traction, condemning the soldiers and accusing them of creating a subculture. The media outrage continued with accusations of war crimes, later disproved.

Historic Norse symbols used by the Telemark Battalion were falsely linked to neo-Nazism. The soldiers felt betrayed by the officials' unjustified accusations: They were warriors. This was their job and they were doing it well.

The media created another controversy over the infantry unit's use of a skull logo inspired by the comic character The Punisher. The furor peaked as then-Lieutenant General Bernt Iver Ferdinand Brovold, in front of invited media, painted over a skull on a vehicle in Camp Nidaros. The vehicle Brovold chose was used for demining; that particular skull was the internationally recognized warning sign for mines. Our military was being led by idiots!

I was stunned by the ignorance and disloyalty of our top military leaders. How in the world could these people oversee soldiers in battle? Luckily, their actions were quickly seen through and public opinion turned against them. Most people back home supported the soldiers and showed compassion for what had been said and done under the pressure of war.

Despite this and my unfulfilling time with the NSE, I wanted to go back to Afghanistan. As soon as I got home I sent another application to the Telemark Battalion, hoping it would be better received this time.

3 CAMP RENA

I enjoy traveling by train. Sitting by the window listening to music, watching the landscape rush by clears my mind. My trip in May 2011 wasn't that serene. As the train steamed through my home territory in Hedmark past the town where I grew up and headed for Rena, a small village in the middle of nowhere, I was way too excited to enjoy the familiar cultivated fields and deep forests I hadn't seen since moving to Oslo six years earlier. My application for the Telemark Battalion had been approved and I was on my way to selection. Passing this examination could transform me from a part-time soldier in the Home Guard to a full-time fighter in the Norwegian Army's most professional unit. It could take me to the Afghan front where I would fulfill my childhood dream of becoming a true warrior.

The competition was tough. More than 550 applicants contended for fifty spots in the battalion and its support companies. Half had been invited to the week-long selection. Many of the hopeful candidates had travelled in my train, easily distinguishable from the rest of the passengers. It's something you learn after a while in the military; hairstyle, clothes, posture and demeanor often reveal a soldier out of uniform.

I studied my rivals. Most, if not all, were younger than me. Many had probably just completed their conscription and were perhaps in better physical condition. I hoped my experience in Afghanistan would give me an advantage, but I would have to give it my all in the coming days. This was my final shot at the Telemark Battalion. This time I couldn't fail. The train ground to a halt at Rena station. There was no organized transport, so we humped our bags the two miles to Camp Rena.

The battalion was proficient at identifying those who could be trained as professional soldiers and those who didn't have it in them. The next week consisted of interviews, informational meetings and a barrage of tests; running tests with and without backpacks, strength tests, swimming tests. We were examined by doctors and interviewed by officers.

It was the stress management test that revealed the most about a candidate. We were rapidly pushed to our physical and mental limits, and it was quickly apparent who among us was aggressive enough, could withstand intense verbal and physical pressure, and could think clearly in high stress situations. I was completely exhausted after the test and could barely stand, but when an instructor asked if I was ready for another round, to my surprise I roared "Yes!" I was not going to show weakness. I was going to fight until my body gave out, and then do more.

The test ended, and I was escorted to a waiting area with other candidates and handed a cardboard cup of water. I could barely lift it to my mouth using both hands. I emptied the cup in one gulp and looked around. The others were also exhausted but exchanging looks of approval and pats on the back. Although we didn't know each other, we had already developed a sense of camaraderie. I wanted more of this feeling. We didn't get any feedback on our performance, but I knew I had given it my all. There was nothing left to do but go home and await a final decision.

Three months later I boarded the same train to Rena. I had passed selection, but I couldn't let my guard down just yet. The six-week basic training course - in practice, boot camp - lay ahead. We had been told this would be the real test of whether we were good enough for the Telemark Battalion. I still had a lot to prove.

"The name is Mike," I said, as I handed my driver's license to the guard at the main gate. He crossed my name off his list and handed me an envelope with a key card and map of the camp with my assigned barracks marked. I found the three-story wooden building, let myself into the first floor and then into what would be my home for the coming years.

The room was simply furnished with a bed, nightstand, desk and chair, a few shelves on the wall and a round coffee table with an armchair. It was small and sterile, much like a typical Norwegian prison cell, I imagined. I didn't mind, though. I was happy to finally be at Rena. Now I just had to get through basic training.

The next six weeks were filled with long days in the field, a lot of marching and drills in the deep pine forests around Rena. During two exercises we didn't sleep or eat for several days. Soldiers fell asleep marching and toppled into a ditch. Others hallucinated, shouting that polar bears were attacking them. One night I asked a bush for directions to the bivouac area. I kept this incident to myself. I developed Achilles tendinitis in both feet, which I thought would end my career.

After six grueling weeks, those who passed the course got our reward, the emerald green beret of the professional Telemark Battalion soldier. I had made it, for now. I was assigned a position as driver in the mortar platoon, a small unit of twenty-eight guys. I knew very little about mortars, but I was excited and ready to learn more about this weapon system.

Some of the platoon had recently returned from Afghanistan and I was eager to hear their experiences. The platoon had been part of the PRT Meymaneh infantry unit and had engaged in several firefights. Their mortars had been very effective against the enemy.

I couldn't wait to deploy, although just months earlier Norway had decided to withdraw its combat troops and pass the infantry's mission to Latvian forces. This was the Norwegian response to increased Taliban activity in Northern Afghanistan. Many considered it cowardly for Norway to leave risky operations to other countries while our soldiers trained local forces in the safety of the camps.

The following year, the government went one step further and pulled Norwegian forces out of PRT Meymaneh and the Faryab province completely. Camp Meymaneh, built from the ground up by Norway, was handed over to Afghan authorities together with the province's security responsibility. Not surprisingly, security in Faryab went from bad to worse after the handover.

"There will always be new missions," the veterans in the platoon told us, and I had to believe them.

After basic training I went on a two-week vehicle course, then I was trained on the mortar, which I would operate as well.

Mortar use became widespread during the First World War and remains relevant in modern warfare against hostile personnel targets. The mortar is a tube secured to a steel plate, supported by a tripod. Grenades are dropped into the tube and shot out with violent force. 81mm grenades have a range of more than three miles and are precise and deadly. The grenade's curved trajectory allows it to hit targets from above so digging oneself into a defensive fighting position doesn't necessarily afford protection. We called this indirect fire, or "death from above."

"Sucks to be on the receiving end as these babies rain down on you," I thought as I studied the grenade in my hand, not knowing that would soon be a part of my everyday life.

After a hectic fall full of training, courses and exercises, it was soon the Christmas holidays. But first we had our bi-annual employee evaluations. I was called into the meeting room where the platoon leader and my team leader sat waiting. The platoon leader spoke first, and his feedback wasn't good.

"Your progress after basic training is below what is expected in an elite unit, Mike," he began. "Your effort has simply not been good enough. Consider this an oral warning. After two oral warnings, you will receive a written warning and then we can fire you."

I was surprised. Admittedly, I was not the platoon's best physical specimen. And it had taken me some time to learn the mortar, but I didn't think I was that bad. That I wasn't the only one in the platoon to receive such a warning was a shock. I had to act. I could not lose my spot now that I had come so far.

In the new year I immersed myself in gaining weight and physical training. I read, I ate and I exercised in my free time, despite beginning every workday with an hour-long workout. I trained every evening and took long runs in the forest and interval runs on the track. I spent hours at a time in the gym.

In my room I devoured instruction manuals for the weapon systems and vehicles we used. While the others traveled home on weekends or went to the local bar, I stayed in camp to run more, lift more and eat more. I would eat until I felt sick. I was going to meet and surpass the unit's high expectations.

The tone of my next evaluation before the summer holiday was quite different. Like many others, the platoon leader had noticed my progress. I was offered responsibility for the platoon's physical training, a great honor. In addition, I was sent to a vehicle instructor course and by autumn, had become the main teacher for new M113 drivers. To be trusted to that extent was humbling.

Although the outlook for deployment abroad was bleak and military service very demanding, I found purpose in my job. I liked the responsibilities, challenges, routines and values in the unit. The Telemark Battalion had the warrior culture I sought. To be aggressive, independent, courageous and hard-tempered was respected rather than looked down on, as it had been with the NSE. I was proud to belong to this unit, proud of my fellow soldiers and proud of my command. There was nothing I wanted more than to go to war with this elite group.

The Telemark Battalion is usually the first to deploy when politicians commit Norwegian soldiers to armed conflict abroad. Therefore, it is essential that its soldiers have the right motivations and accept the risk involved. Most Telemark applicants want to deploy abroad and many desire combat experience.

During selection, applicants are asked if they are willing to go abroad. If not, or if they can't kill in combat, they are advised to consider another profession. Telemark soldiers spend a lot of time training for the violence of war, learning to kill as effectively as possible. Each and every one of us invested significant time and health to get good at exactly this - killing other humans. We talked about this often. I think most of us knew that war brings misery and suffering, but the reality that we could face foreign barbarism at home if it wasn't stopped abroad couldn't be ignored.

Frost injuries were common from endless days honing our skills in all kinds of weather and wind. Repetitive strain injuries were rampant from extreme exercise.

Is it then not natural to want to use our hard-earned skills in a real situation? Some compare preparation for war to football: If a team trains hard, year after year, but never tests its skills against a real opponent, the players become frustrated.

War illuminates the darkest side of human nature. Think of the ravages of the Mongols, the fall of Constantinople or the Holocaust. Hidden under our civility we are still animals, and survival of the fittest is the brutal truth that many people in safe Norway have either not realized or simply deny.

As I saw it, I had to be prepared to meet this animal face to face one day. This reality motivated me when I was hungry, cold or tired of all the training. But the more we trained, the more I wanted to test of my skills in combat, in the face of the beast. Many others were similarly driven.

Unfortunately, Telemark received only training missions. In January 2013, the battalion's tank squadron and one of the battalion's two mechanized infantry companies were assigned to support the Afghan police in Mazar-i-Sharif with training and counseling for one year. No one from my platoon went and, based on reports from those who did, we didn't miss out on much.

"The mission was bullshit," said Matthias, my barracks neighbor, after returning home after six months in Mazar-i-Sharif. "We spent most of our time in camp doing nothing sensible. The Afghans were not interested in training."

It seemed our politicians were no longer willing to risk Norwegian lives abroad, and that future missions would take place only in low-risk areas.

In the summer of 2013, our hope revived. Because of the ongoing Syrian civil war, Austria withdrew its troops from the UN observer force on the Golan Heights between Israel and Syria. The security situation had turned severe; many UN soldiers had been kidnapped by Syrian rebels. The UN asked Sweden to take over the mission. Sweden agreed on the condition that the other Scandinavian countries participate. Norway rejected the request and the joint Scandinavian force fizzled. The hope of a new, meaningful mission faded as fast as it arrived.

In Norway, a professional soldier signs a contract for three years at a time but, as in any other job, can quit at will with three-months' notice.

Before the 2014 summer holiday my contract was almost over, my future awaited and I attended my final employee evaluation. My platoon leader said I was among the most trusted in the platoon and my heart swelled with pride. When he asked if I would sign a new contract, I answered with a definitive "Yes!" Over the next three years I could take courses, financed by the military, that would better equip me for a civilian job after my military career. Although I was very fond of life in Rena, regulations limit the length of professional military service and I had to prepare for civilian life. So I signed my second contract and looked forward to three more years in the battalion.

That summer I took a two-week maritime security course in Florida. It was difficult for Norwegians to get a foot inside the international security industry, where big money could be made as armed guards on cargo ships and gas and oil rigs in the more troubled parts of the world. I hoped the courses I took would increase my chances of landing such a job.

Then ISIS rolled through Iraq and my world was turned upside down.

4 PRELUDE TO WAR

In the summer of 2014, I watched in horror as ISIS ravaged the Kurdish Region. At one point, the Islamists were just eighteen miles from Erbil, Iraq's Kurdish capitol. Kurdish authorities were not prepared for the ISIS offensive, and in several places Peshmerga forces retreated or fled in panic; the Americans eventually came to their rescue. Intense air strikes stopped the advancing Islamists and gave the Peshmerga time to reorganize and strike back.

It was soon clear the Telemark Battalion would not take an active role in the war against ISIS. At home, there was no political will to use force against the terrorist group, although more than a hundred Norwegian citizens had joined ISIS and could pose a real threat to the country if they returned home. I felt a burning need to do something, but what?

I thought about what Dilshad had said earlier. Was it possible to go to Iraq on our own and join the Peshmerga? We had read about Norwegian Kurds who had travelled there to fight, but neither Dilshad nor I knew anyone in Norway's Kurdish community we could ask for help. Nor did we have any network or acquaintances in the country of our birth. We agreed to investigate what opportunities we had.

I also wanted to involve Eivind, Anders and Frank, three friends from my squadron. As ethnic Norwegians they perhaps lacked the burning motivation that gripped Dilshad and me, but I knew them well and knew they might be interested. It would feel safer to travel with more people we could trust one hundred percent and these three were solid.

Eivind had worked in the mortar platoon for several years and had seen combat in Afghanistan. After a recent knee injury, he had switched to the medical platoon and quickly became one of the unit's best medics. Eivind's mindset was similar to my own and he was perhaps the guy I trusted the most in the whole battalion.

Anders was in my platoon. Although relatively young and inexperienced, he was intelligent, serious and mature. He had an educated understanding of the Middle East conflict. I didn't need cowboys looking for action, I needed men who understood our motivation and what we wanted to achieve.

Frank was also in the medical platoon and a good friend with whom I spent a lot of time outside work. He was hardcore, well-trained and the only one in the squadron who did more pullups than me, to my great annoyance. I pitched the idea and Eivind and Anders were interested. I had my team.

I had planned to immediately introduce Eivind and Anders to Dilshad, but that fall my platoon had several extended exercises, so we put our plans on hold. After a week training in Hedmark, one and a half weeks in Northern Norway and almost four weeks on the East Coast of the US without access to phone or the Internet, we finally returned to Rena. Much had happened in the meantime.

During the September NATO summit in Wales, the US had gathered nine allied nations at a meeting where it established a coalition to defeat ISIS militarily. Norway had not been invited. To many, Norway's Solberg government appeared unresponsive and passive. Less than two weeks later, Norway announced it would send five staff officers to a UN meeting in Tampa, Florida, to help plan the coalition's military efforts in Iraq. It was rumored that Norway's government was considering a military presence in Iraq, without further details.

In October, heads of defense from twenty-two countries were invited to a military summit in Washington D.C. Norway's then chief of defense, Haakon Bruun-Hanssen, was not; embarrassing for a government that had long positioned itself as an important NATO supporter and US ally. It was clear that sending staff to Florida had not been enough.

I was increasingly sure that if I wanted to contribute directly in the war against ISIS, my team would have to go on its own. In November I gathered them for the first time at a couple of secret meetings to discuss our strategy. Planning unsanctioned travel to a war zone was a challenge. We had heard of Western citizens joining Peshmerga forces in Northern Iraq and the Kurdish YPG militia in Syria. We turned to social media to find them.

I scoured Facebook and Instagram for Western volunteers who had made their way down and taken part in combat. To my great frustration, those I located were either unwilling to help or were not as they appeared. Some were not even in the Middle East but were engaged in various forms of fraud.

The situation deteriorated when, one by one, the rest of the team pulled out. The Norwegian government had finally decided to deploy sixty soldiers to Erbil in the spring of 2015 to train Peshmerga forces. Which unit had not yet been decided, but since the Telemark Battalion was the logical choice, Dilshad, Eivind and Anders decided to stay put in the hope of deploying with this force.

I was disappointed, but I understood and respected their choices. It was, after all, the most reasonable thing to do. Why quit their secure jobs and risk future military opportunities on a trip that might well fail? The volunteer community in Iraq seemed unreliable. My team would risk traveling to Erbil or Sulaymaniyah only to find that whoever was supposed to help us never showed up at the airport. If we did find our way to the front on our own, they could easily be injured or killed. It was far more reasonable to deploy with the armed forces, train others to fight and stay out of battle. They would return to their loved ones in one piece, earn a lot of money, and receive medals and pats on the back after the mission ended.

What was I to do? Should I make the reasonable choice like my friends? Or should I follow my heart and travel to the Kurdish Region as a foreign fighter with all its danger and uncertainty? I have since learned I'm not always the best at making reasonable choices.

MIKE PESHMERGANOR

5 THE HARD CHOICE

There was much to support abandoning my plans to go to Iraq on my own. But what kind of mission would Norwegian forces really get in Erbil? I interpreted Norway's military presence as part of a political game. Our government wanted to claim it had troops on the ground in Iraq, without our soldiers really making a difference. Their goal, as I saw it, was to be visible, preferably in a place outside any real danger.

I guessed the upcoming mission would look very much like Telemark's last Afghanistan assignment to train unmotivated police officers in Mazar-i-Sharif. I knew Afghans and Kurds had many cultural similarities, and I surmised the Norwegian instructors in Erbil would face many of the same challenges my barracks neighbor Mathias had experienced in Mazar-i-Sharif the prior year. If I deployed with the armed forces, I would most likely come home feeling I had achieved nothing of value, as I had after the Afghanistan deployment. It was a difficult choice for many reasons, but after many rounds with myself, I realized I had to go down on my own.

I spent a lot of time in the barracks' communal kitchen and TV lounge. After my evening workout, I cooked dinner and ate with Frank while we watched the news and discussed current events. Our conclusion was consistent: The world was going to Hell. One night I sat alone in the TV lounge long after Frank had gone to bed. I had dishes to clean but I was exhausted after a long day of work and training, so I picked up my phone and opened Instagram.

One of my biggest challenges was finding a reliable contact in Northern Iraq who could help me into a Peshmerga unit. I scrolled through Instagram posts and stopped at an image of a young man in uniform in front of an armored vehicle bearing a Kurdish flag. I had seen countless such photos on social media, but something about this picture stood out; I couldn't pinpoint exactly what. The person who had posted the photo was a

German Kurd named Agit who, like many other Kurds from Europe, had recently joined the fight against the Islamists. I sent him a message asking for his help. It was a shot in the dark, but to my surprise he was willing.

All I had to do was get to Erbil and Agit would fix the rest. I had been promised this by many others, but as I got to know Agit over the coming weeks I came to believe I could count on him. I had my contact. Now I had to prepare for the trip.

The first step was to quit my job. But how to do so without arousing suspicion? Just a few months earlier I had signed a new three-year contract. To quit now I needed a believable explanation that was far from the truth. I feared being exposed. I feared the Norwegian Police Security Service, or PST, would somehow prevent me from leaving Norway.

Steeling myself, I knocked on my platoon leader's door. I told him a close family member was ill and I had to terminate my contract to be a caregiver for a period. He was understanding and seemed genuinely sorry for my situation. It was December and I would have to work through my three months' notice until the beginning of April. But I had a good deal of vacation days and overtime, so he said I could most likely leave in mid-February. I would be welcome back anytime. I thanked the him and left the office. He had been an exceptional platoon leader and had put an incredible amount of trust in me during the last years. I felt bad lying to him.

The hardest part lay ahead. Now I had to tell my girlfriend and my parents that I was going to war, again. This time alone.

I had been with Susanne for a little more than a year. Although I was several years older than she, we quickly hit it off. There was something remarkable about her, an innocence I had almost forgotten existed. She made me feel things I didn't know I could, both good and bad. Before half a year passed she heard the three words I had never said to anyone: "I love you."

Nevertheless, I was willing to sacrifice our relationship, like everything else, by leaving. I assumed she would break up with me once I revealed my plan.

"Why should I break up?" She asked. "I'm proud of you for wanting to make a difference."

Tears filled my eyes. She knew I would be gone for several months. Perhaps I would not come home whole, or at all. Yet she was willing to wait for me. It spoke loads about her faith in our relationship. But did she realize how hard this would be? Did I?

My parents didn't take the news as well. My father, grandfather and grandmother had been in the resistance against the Iraqi regime, so I hoped they, more than anyone, would understand my decision. I understood their fear. In the last year, ISIS had aired several grotesque execution videos. Prisoners of war and kidnapping victims were killed on camera in the most brutal ways imaginable. Naturally my parents didn't want to watch their son getting his head cut off with a blunt knife.

I knew captivity at the hands of ISIS was far worse than death. I wasn't afraid of being taken prisoner. If I was ever in that situation I was prepared to take my own life. I knew I could do it. I didn't tell my parents this. Rather, I reassured them that, given my background and experience, I would probably be placed far from the front line to train other soldiers.

In truth, I wanted to be as far forward as possible, and among the first to enter Mosul and deprive ISIS of its self-declared Iraqi capital. I wanted to kick down the doors, go in first and come out victorious from every battle or die trying. I wanted to punish the enemy. Reports of ISIS' crimes in Syria and Iraq were almost too cruel to comprehend.

In December, the radicals had distributed leaflets to the residents of Mosul announcing it was now legal to hold non-Muslim girls as sex slaves and sell them as property.

"It is allowed to have intercourse with a female slave who is not in puberty yet, if she is fit for sexual intercourse. If she is a virgin, the owner can have sexual intercourse with her immediately. If she is not a virgin, her womb must be cleaned." I promised myself that if I encountered anyone who, without reasonable doubt, had participated in the sale of slaves, sexual abuse of women and children, or torture and killings of prisoners, I would show no mercy.

The Christmas holiday arrived, and I spent my time at home industriously. I started purchasing the long list of equipment I needed: Bags, backpacks, knives, gloves, belts, holster, GPS, watch and gun cleaning equipment from a military store; two sets of the best uniform on the market and a ballistic helmet; hiking equipment and shoes; clothes and hearing protection in a sports shop; a bullet-proof plate carrier vest from abroad. Nothing was to be left to chance when it came to equipment. I spent almost $5,000 in a matter of weeks. If the equipment I bought could increase my combat endurance or effectiveness, the price didn't matter.

In the shed at home I spray-painted the black helmet in desert camouflage and mounted a helmet camera, which were popular at Rena to evaluate one's own and others' performance during training exercises. I thought it would be useful in war too.

The armed forces made sure we got everything we needed in terms of clothing, equipment and medical examinations before a deployment. This time I was my own. I got vaccines and booked dental and medical appointments, saying I was going abroad for a long time and needed a thorough check of my teeth and general health.

I had a lot to do, but I also had time to celebrate Christmas and New Year's with Susanne. We spent Christmas Eve at my apartment, just the two of us. We baked gingerbread and watched Christmas movies. I dreaded saying goodbye to her in February and hoped we could celebrate Christmas again next year.

Back at Rena after the holidays my plans were ready to kick off. As expected, the Telemark Battalion received orders to send a force to Northern Iraq to train the Peshmerga. The platoon was called in to a meeting announcing that the first force would consist mostly of soldiers from the cavalry squadron. The combat support squadron, of which my platoon was a part, would assist and provide support functions such as medics, communications, logistics and mortar training. The first contingent would deploy in early April and spend four months in Erbil. Our platoon would send four men, a choice based on efforts in daily service, seniority and skills relevant to the mission.

The room was thick with anticipation as we waited to hear the four names. Given my seniority and language skills, it was likely I would have been chosen had I not terminated my contract.

"Patrick will be team leader," our platoon leader intoned. "Mats is second in command. Lasse, forward observer and Rune, driver. To everyone else, there will be new opportunities when the platoon supports the third contingent with another team in less than a year. That is all."

Many disappointed faces left the meeting room. Four tried to hide their excitement as best they could. I was happy on their behalf, the four skilled guys. But I didn't envy them. I had a clear picture of how their mission would pan out, and I knew I had made the right choice.

"You will regret you left when you find out we've wiped out a whole squad of ISIS fighters with our mortars down in Iraq, Mike," Mats laughed.

"If you only knew," I thought and laughed back.

Dilshad would deploy as an interpreter and, like Mats and some of the others in the battalion, believed he might end up fighting Islamists.

"Maybe they'll use us for more than just training when the offensive to take back Mosul starts," Dilshad said. "It will be a massive operation, and I doubt the Iraqis and Peshmerga will make it alone."

Dilshad had a point. But I was still not convinced Norway would participate in offensive operations.

Eivind was also going as part of the medical team and Anders hoped to deploy with the third contingent, so I made no further attempts to recruit him.

I continued my preparations in secret. I identified the equipment I could keep after leaving, like my sleeping bag, sleeping pad and boots, and swapped them for brand new ones. I hoarded expiring field rations. One night, Frank and I snuck out and filled a garbage bag with medical supplies from one of the medical platoon's containers. I felt ready for the journey.

Friday, February 13 was my last day at work. As on every Friday, we would start the day doing interval training with the rest of the squadron. We waited outside the garage for the squadron chief's brief before the session began.

"Mike, step forward!" the chief commanded. Surprised, I walked to his left side and faced the squadron at parade rest with my legs shoulder-width apart and my hands folded behind my back. The chief told everyone that I was quitting, and why. He praised my efforts and achievements during the past three and a half years, saying he hoped to see me back in the squadron as soon as possible. He handed me a plaque with the unit's symbol - a Viking ship - as thanks for my service.

A wave of conscience washed over me as I looked at the assembly. I wished I could have been honest about my mission. I felt terrible lying to my colleagues, but I didn't see any other way. I took the plaque, shook the chief's hand, and returned to my place. On the way out, Anders and I exchanged looks and he gave an approving nod. I hoped the others would also understand my choice.

MIKE PESHMERGANOR

6 THE ROAD TO THE FRONT

It was obvious I wasn't going on holiday as I walked into Gardermoen airport on February 23, with two large bags of military equipment and tactical gear, a backpack, a laptop and other civilian kit. I worried that I would be questioned by customs after check-in, and the PST notified. Could I be mistaken for a jihadist foreign fighter?

I had no idea which Peshmerga unit I would be joining, where they were stationed or under what conditions they were living. I had packed enough clothes and equipment to survive with little outside support for a long time. I checked my luggage and passed through the security check without issue. My bags weighed ninety pounds total. It cost more than $120 just to get them on the plane, but that was no surprise. Now I just had to kill a couple of hours, hoping I wouldn't hear my name over the intercom or be stopped at boarding.

Several Norwegian Kurds had travelled to Syria and Iraq to fight ISIS before me. Although it was legal under Norwegian law to join the Kurdish forces, it was not without problems, according to the Norwegian Police Security Service, or PST. In addition, I technically still worked for the Norwegian Army, so I fell into a different category than my predecessors. I feared the authorities would seize my passport or apply some distorted travel ban and I would be discredited, unemployed and stuck with thousands of dollars of unneeded military equipment. I found an airport restaurant and ordered my last meal on Norwegian soil. There was no turning back now.

This was what I had trained for my entire adult life. I was prepared for whatever awaited me in Iraq. I pulled out the dog tag Susanne had given me for my birthday a few weeks earlier. It was engraved "Wherever you are, whatever you do, I'll be here, waiting for you," her promise to me before I left. In return, I had promised to come home alive, a promise that could be difficult to keep.

It was essential my mission remain unknown at the stopover in Istanbul. Turkey was unfriendly to the Kurdish; were my plan to fight ISIS discovered, I would probably be interrogated and even sent home. It was a poorly kept secret that Turkey, a NATO member, let thousands of foreign fighters cross its border into Syria to join ISIS and other terrorist groups. Turkish intelligence covertly provided these groups with military, economic and logistical support.

I hefted my backpack onto the security conveyor. The guard behind the X-ray machine immediately saw something he deemed suspicious and waved a colleague over. Together they studied the computer screen, giving me mistrustful, sidelong looks.

What the hell did I forget to take out? The same backpack had made it through security at Gardermoen without any problem. The guards told me to remove the contents of one of the compartments. I had completely forgotten about the hiking cutlery, a spoon, fork, and knife so blunt it could barely cut butter. The men removed the knife from its carabiner and studied it carefully while discussing in Turkish.

"It's fine, I don't really need the knife," I said nervously. To my relief they confiscated it and allowed me to move on without further examination. I would avoid future stopovers in Turkey, even if it cost more and took longer.

I boarded the next plane, the final leg of my journey to Iraq and the unknown.

I landed in Erbil the night of February 23 and entered the grand and beautiful arrival hall. Had I not known better, I would have thought I was in a wealthy Gulf State.

Following the 2003 US-led invasion of Iraq, the Kurds had become fairly autonomous in three of the country's northernmost provinces. Together, they constitute what many call Kurdistan, or the Kurdish Region. The Kurdish Region was probably the only place in the Middle East where portraits of George W. Bush graced café walls and American flags were sold in the markets. Although the Kurds had not yet declared independence from Iraq, the Kurdish region functioned independently with its own armed forces, health and education departments, government and most hallmarks of a sovereign country except a currency and passport.

Erbil, the capitol, profited from huge oil revenues, to which the opulent airport attested. From the 2003 invasion through the autumn of

2014, when oil prices dropped on the international markets and ISIS began its campaign of death in Northern Iraq, the Kurdish region experienced unprecedented economic growth. Erbil had been widely predicted to become the new Dubai. Now the region, like the rest of the country, was in economic crisis.

A security checkpoint with three guards and an X-ray machine stood at the end of the entry hall. Most passengers were waved through. I don't know if it was my beard, which many Kurds associate with Islamists, but I was singled out for inspection. The guard's eyes widened as he opened my bags and found uniforms, knives, a plate carrier, gas mask and helmet.

"What is this?" he demanded in Sorani, the same Kurdish dialect I had grown up around in Norway. Before the trip, I had worried about my language skills. Although I could understand and speak some Sorani, I knew the various Kurdish dialects were like completely different languages. Fortunately, Sorani was the most common dialect in Erbil. I explained my situation to the guard as best I could.

After investigating my baggage further and ensuring my story's credibility, I got a green light to move on, minus the vest and its ballistic plates.

"You can't bring plates like these in without government approval," the guard said. "We'll take them until you can prove you are allowed to have them."

It made no sense. I felt my frustration coming to a boil. The vest and plates were some of my most important equipment! But I didn't want to argue on my first day in this country. I hoped I could get them back, one way or another. I took my bags outside and found a cab into the city.

Erbil is enormous with highways, tall buildings and big billboards. Dawn was approaching as I entered the city, but the streets were still empty. It was humbling to drive through what felt like a ghost town. I was back in my country of birth. I suddenly felt very alone and very far from home.

The cab driver took me to Ankawa, a Christian district where I had booked a reasonably-priced hotel room. I checked in and immediately fell asleep. After a few hours' rest and a quick shower, I returned to the lobby and settled into one of several sofas. My contact, Agit, had promised to come by with further instructions on joining my unit. The receptionist brought me a cup of tea, and I logged onto the wireless network with my phone to kill time. One of the last things I had done before boarding my plane at Gardermoen was to post a cryptic message on Instagram: "Strong walls are not made of stone, but brave men." The guys at Rena would discover where I was eventually, so I figured I might as well give them this hint. From what I could see, no one had responded.

A black SUV pulled up outside and two men stepped out and headed for the main entrance. This had to be Agit, I thought, and put my phone away. We greeted each other and Agit introduced me to his bodyguard,

Samad. Agit was only nineteen, but seemed educated and, like his older bodyguard, was well groomed and dressed.

"I'm glad I got to meet you, Mike," he said. "I'm flying back to Germany in a few hours and I don't know when I'll return."

Agit had spent five months in an artillery unit and was going home, his duty done. I wondered why he had his own bodyguard, until I learned he was a nephew of the Kurdish president, Masoud Barzani. I was stunned. We had talked for several weeks without his disclosing his relationship to the most powerful Kurdish Region leader.

We quickly hit it off as he told me where his unit had fought. He proudly showed me pictures on his phone of dead enemies, ISIS fighters killed in battle. I hoped I could return to Norway with such mementos. Agit told me about the unit in which he had arranged a spot for me.

"It's led by Wahed Kovle, one of the most famous and fearless Peshmerga generals," Agit said, smiling. "He is a former hitman and was in jail for murder, but now leads his own small unit in Duhok.

"He is currently fighting in Sinjar where he spreads fear among the jihadists. He is totally crazy, but I think you'll fit well in his unit."

"I'm sure I will," I replied. I was entering a world where a former hitman and convicted killer could become a general and command his own military unit. I realized I had a lot to learn about the Kurds.

After exchanging phone numbers with Samad, who would be my contact from now on, I thanked Agit and wished him a safe trip home. Samad promised to call in a few days with further instructions. I returned to my room to digest the conversation.

I had heard about the battles in Sinjar. Urban military operations are among the most demanding. The Syrian civil war had forced the Norwegian military to realize it must master this form of warfare. Conflicts of the future would most likely take place in cities and other densely populated areas. During the last couple years at Rena, we had trained heavily, and realistically, for urban combat. But no matter how well trained or superior a force is, big losses are the expectation.

A wave of adrenaline rushed through me and my hands began to tremble, a reaction I had never experienced before, not even in Afghanistan. I was going to be thrown into the meat grinder, and I looked forward to it.

I spent most of the next days exploring Ankawa while I waited for Samad to call. I went out during the day to eat and become proficient with my new GPS. I quickly became familiar with this part of Erbil. I made daily excursions to the city's few ATMs to withdraw the maximum allowable US dollars which, with Iraqi dinars, were the country's two valid currencies. I had brought US dollars from Norway, so after a few days I had amassed about $9,000 in cash. I anticipated having to buy my own guns and ammunition and I knew black market prices would be astronomical with war's high demand.

Back at the hotel, I inspected my clothes and equipment again to ensure everything was present and in working order. With Samad's help, I had reclaimed my plate carrier and ballistic plates. Days passed, and I grew impatient. Samad was having trouble contacting the general and I began to wonder if Agit had promised more than he could deliver. My parents called several times a day begging me to come home. My mother cried as she recounted dreams in which I was burned alive in a cage.

A few weeks earlier, ISIS had broadcast footage of a Jordanian F-16 pilot captured after his jet crashed near Raqqa, ISIS' self-declared Syrian capital. In the video, 26-year-old Math Al-Kasasbeh, wearing the characteristic orange prisoner jumpsuit, is forced into a small steel cage. A prideful terrorist ignites the cage and flames engulf Muath as horrified viewers witnessed his slow, agonizing death.

Shortly thereafter, ISIS broadcast another video, this time of twenty-one captured orange-clad Peshmerga soldiers crammed into similar cages and paraded through the Iraqi city of Hawija. Cheering Sunnis line the streets and it was implied the prisoners would meet the same fate as the Jordanian pilot. My parents were distraught. I had some rough days, knowing I was subjecting those I loved at home to intense fear.

My hotel bill grew. I became paranoid. I worried about the hotel staff, who turned out to be Arab. I slept with a chair under the door handle and my folding knife under my pillow in case the staff informed on me to their ISIS friends or others who could profit from abducting me. Nevertheless, I remained determined to find my way to the front. I began considering Syria and the Kurdish YPG militia as a backup plan.

After a week, Samad finally called. He had spoken to the general, who was at home in Duhok waiting for me. The next day I headed west in a cab with my gear. I was excited and relieved to leave Erbil.

The most direct route from Erbil to Duhok would have taken us through Mosul. For obvious reasons we had to avoid the ISIS-held city, and after two hours we safely arrived at our destination. Duhok is a medium-sized city surrounded by mountains, its streets full of life. My driver stopped the first cab we encountered and asked for direction to the general's home.

Wahed Kovle was obviously a celebrity and the local cabbie immediately offered to show us the way, for a small fee. He led us to a large house in the city center surrounded by tall walls and armed guards who informed us the general was not at home, but at the Tel Skuf front.

Another delay.

I was confused. Where was Tel Skuf? Shouldn't the general be in Sinjar? My driver wouldn't go to the front. He seemed nervous about the road ahead. The local driver offered to take me for thirty thousand dinars, or just over twenty-five dollars. We set our course toward this unknown place called Tel Skuf. I questioned the new driver about my destination, but communication was difficult: The local dialect, Badini, is nothing like Sorani.

Leaving Duhok, we passed a sign indicating we were driving towards Mosul. Anxiety gripped me. I gripped the folding knife in my thigh pocket and immediately calmed. Dusk settled on the desolate plains as we passed signs announcing "Mosul 43 kilometers." "Mosul 36 kilometers." "Mosul 32 kilometers."

"Fuck! This has to stop soon," I thought. I looked at my driver, a big, burly guy. If he made an unexpected stop near a bunch of bearded men with rifles, I would have no problem running my knife through his throat first. There were Kurds in ISIS' ranks, and Kurdish sympathizers; I had no guarantee my driver wasn't one.

After almost an hour, we reached the village of Tel Skuf and I breathed a heavy sigh of relief. The small town was dark, and I saw no civilians, only a few soldiers and military vehicles.

"We must be very close to the front line," I thought.

We drove through Tel Skuf past multiple check points until the road ended at a long, man-made earthen berm a few miles outside town. The long journey was finally over. I was at Mosul's front line.

BLOOD MAKES THE GRASS GROW

7 THOSE WHO FACE DEATH

The Kurdish front in Iraq was almost 800 miles long, stretching east from the Syrian border towards Iran. It was defended by the Peshmerga, directly translated as "those who face death." Historically, the Peshmerga has been a loose network of discrete groups fighting for Kurdish rights, but at times against each other. Recent attempts to unify the independent militia under one command and build a regular military structure have met with mixed results.

The front line was marked by a trench several yards deep and wide built to prevent the enemy from breaking through with vehicles. Behind the trench, "positions" manned by a handful of soldiers each, were dug at regular intervals into a six-foot-high berm of compacted soil. Between the trench and the berm, streetlights illuminated the trench and some of no man's land, an open field controlled by neither side.

In reality, and to Iraq's great frustration, the front line is the border between the Kurdish Region and the rest of Iraq. Iraq claims the Kurds used the war as an excuse to establish a physical border with the rest of the country, including disputed areas. Many expect this to ignite a new conflict after ISIS is destroyed.

A couple of soldiers helped me carry my bags from the cab. From where I stood, I could see the lights along the front twist snake-like across the mountain several miles to the east. It was an impressive sight.

I was led to an unfinished two-story concrete structure close to the berm, used by the soldiers as shelter.

"The general will meet you soon. Do you want tea while you wait?" one of the soldiers asked. Tea is an important part of Kurdish culture. It's unthinkable to hold meetings, entertain guests or simply socialize with friends without serving hot tea, often in small glass cups with such enormous amounts of sugar that it's rare to meet Kurds older than thirty with all their teeth.

Nearly two hours and several cups of tea later, the general finally appeared with a large entourage. The soldiers' posture immediately changed. There was no doubt he was the boss, the alpha male.

General Kovli was in his mid-forties, wore a well-trimmed beard and was short, like most Kurds, but with the sharp, intense look of authority. He seemed angry as he shouted commands in a hoarse whiskey voice, gesturing in all directions. He approached me and I nervously thanked him in bad Kurdish for accepting me into his unit. He smiled and bid me welcome before shouting more orders to the soldiers, who promptly threw my bags into a pickup truck.

We headed back toward Tel Skuf along the same road I had travelled just a few hours earlier. Why were we headed away from the front? I thought I would be stationed at the front line with the rest of the soldiers! Was I being stationed safely away from the front line because I knew the president's nephew? Before I could ask, the truck took a sharp right into a small village a few hundred yards from the front line.

"Welcome to Baqofah, your new home," the driver said.

Like Tel Skuf, Baqofah was blacked out and appeared abandoned. We drove down a street past three houses that appeared inhabited and parked beyond the furthest one. The driver honked, and two soldiers ran out and disappeared back into the house with my bags as quickly as they had come. A soldier in his early twenties approached and introduced himself as Saad in fluent Sorani. I was relieved I could communicate with someone in my own dialect.

I followed Saad into the house, comprised of a living room, kitchen, two bedrooms, toilet, bathroom and another living room on the second floor. The house had belonged to an Assyrian family forced to flee with the rest of the village when ISIS arrived. Assyrians are Christians with a long history in the Middle East. Over time, religious and ethnic conflicts have forced many Assyrians t
o abandon their traditional homeland. More than 120,000 Assyrians now call Sweden home. Their football club, Assyriska, plays at the top level.

"We have made a bed for you. Do you want to change?" Saad asked as he led me to one of the bedrooms. I was still wearing civilian clothes. The tiny bedroom held six beds; the one in the corner, with bright pink sheets, was mine. I changed into my uniform and followed Saad to the living room to meet the rest of the unit.

Almost twenty soldiers lived in the house and most were gathered in front of the TV. Saad introduced me, and I could feel the men measuring me. They spoke Badini and although I couldn't understand their words, I felt their skepticism instantly. I guess they thought I was just another war tourist, here to post pictures from the front on Facebook then return to Norway and the good life.

"I'll show you," I thought. I accepted another cup of tea and found a place on the sofa next to Saad, who told me more about my new unit.

"We are around four hundred men in total; most are at the front line you visited tonight," he said. "Here in Bagofah, we are about twenty-five men split between this house and the neighboring one, where the general lives when he is at the front.

"We are the Quick Reaction Force and the general's entourage. We also have two houses in Tel Skuf for administration offices and storage. Half the force is at the front at any given time. We serve for one week then spend one week off at home." I nodded.

"What's the Quick Reaction Force's job?" I asked. Saad explained that we moved to the front line during attacks and heightened preparedness or to fill empty positions. We would also escort the general when he traveled, whether to official meetings or to visit his family in Duhok.

"He has many enemies because of his past," Saad whispered, looking around to ensure no one had overheard. It was clear the general's history as a hitman was a sensitive subject.

"What about Sinjar?" I asked.

"The general was there with a small group for almost three months, but our mission was recently terminated," Saad said. "I was there for several weeks; it was intense. We threw grenades and shot at Daesh at close range. We were so close to Daesh we could curse at them." He laughed, slapping his thigh. Daesh is a derogatory term for ISIS, popular in the Middle East. ISIS cuts out the tongues of those caught using the word.

I was angry at myself for missing Sinjar but gratified that I was finally at the front. New opportunities would come.

The next morning, I joined my unit in the kitchen, sitting on the floor as is customary, for a breakfast of flatbread sprinkled with water to soften it, yogurt, tahini, a syrup made of dates and, of course, tea. The guys tore pieces of flatbread, dunked them in a mixture of tahini and syrup or yoghurt, and washed it down with a sip of tea. I followed their example.

After breakfast, I trailed Saad to the guard post outside the general's house. Several men sat on guard, drinking tea and talking. The atmosphere was relaxed and it was clear the post was also a place for socializing. Saad proudly showed me a picture of his newborn daughter on his phone and I wondered if I'd be willing to risk my life at the front if I were a father. I had great respect for my fellow soldiers, all of whom had volunteered to fight ISIS.

I heard a faint thud in the distance. No one else seemed to notice. Another thud followed a few minutes later, this time much closer.

"Saad, wasn't that an explosion?" I asked, confused.

"Yes, Daesh shoots at us with mortars and rockets from the next village daily," he answered casually, as he stirred his tea. I smiled, recalling Afghanistan, where rockets landing several hundred yards outside the Norwegian camp in Mazar-i-Sharif caused newspaper headlines at home. Here, it was barely a blip on the screen. A flimsy, middle-aged man with a moustache emerged from the general's house and addressed me in fluent Swedish.

Ghasem, the general's cook, had lived many years in Sweden before moving back to Duhok to help his father run their family restaurant. He handed me an energy drink and told me to follow him for a tour of the village. "Wild Tiger Energy Drink" adorned the can above a leaping tiger. The drink was produced locally and after a single sip I knew I would get addicted.

"If I'm not killed in battle, I'll die of diabetes," I thought.

I followed Ghasem into the small village, where old mud houses perched on narrow streets crossing left and right. Except for the three somewhat modern houses in our street, most of the structures seemed old enough to be mistaken for an archaeological site.

We climbed onto the roof of an old church for a better view. The front line was seven- to eight-hundred yards away, and I could see the house where I had awaited the general the evening before. On the roof was a guard post I hadn't seen in the dark, with soldiers pacing restlessly back and forth.

"Our area of responsibility starts at that house and stretches four- to five-hundred yards west," Ghasem explained in Swedish. "The rest of the line is manned by another unit."

"How often is this front attacked?" I asked, finishing off the Wild Tiger.

"Rarely, but they shoot at us daily from Batnaya, the town you see over there," he said, pointing to a small town about two miles south with a large, distinctive water tower topped by a black flag.

"It must be that fucking ISIS flag," I thought.

Ghasem explained that our job was to make sure ISIS couldn't break through the front. Only when the Mosul offensive began were we to head south and take Batnaya, then Tel Keppe and finally Mosul itself.

I couldn't believe my luck. Not only was I stationed near Mosul, but I was in a unit that would help liberate the city! The idea of taking the capital from ISIS excited me.

We descended from the roof and inspected some of the abandoned houses. The inhabitants of this and nearby areas had fled in a single night. Clothes, books, photographs, and cosmetics lay scattered around. It was clear the houses had been searched for valuables.

"Daesh controlled Baqofah and Tel Skuf for two weeks last fall before we pushed them back to Batnaya," Ghasem said as he rifled a chest of drawers. I suspected ISIS weren't the only looters.

Later that day I met Roj, the general's son. He was young but highly respected by the men. Now that his father had gone home to Duhok, Roj was in charge. He sent me with a driver to Tel Skuf to collect an AK-47 rifle from storage. The AK-47 is an automatic rifle developed by the Soviet Union in the late '40s. It was designed for easy use and maintenance, but at the expense of accuracy, which I was soon to experience. The AK-47 is popular in the third world due to its availability and low price. That the AK-47 is featured on the Mozambique flag attests to this weapon's importance.

Back in Baqofah, Roj and I had a shooting contest. I used my AK-47 against Roj's American M16 rifle. We placed bottles against a brick wall as targets and I lost big time. I asked Roj to try his rifle, with its attached optical sight.

"Here, shoot the street lights," he said. I aimed the M16 at the closest one. A loud metallic "ping" sounded against the steel pole. I aimed for the next pole, farther away, squeezed the trigger, and was rewarded with another ping. I continued until I had hit every pole to the end of the street without a miss. The guys were impressed.

"We really appreciate having someone with your experience," Roj said as I handed back his weapon. "If you need anything, do not hesitate to ask."

"Maybe someone can drive me to Duhok someday to buy my own M16 and a pistol?" My rifle in the Norwegian armed forces, the HK416, is a modern version of the M16, so I more or less knew this weapon. It was also easier to mount optical sights on the M16, critical in my eyes. I guessed fighting at this front would happen at long range, and the AK-47's old iron sights would be of little use.

The next day another relative of the general's drove me to Duhok. Waled was a civilian and the unit's errand boy, a role assigned to him as punishment for beating up his mother drunk. He drove to the city center and parked at a small square where a group of older men sat on benches smoking water pipes and drinking tea. Waled, who spoke some English, told me to sit on one of the benches, then shouted at a little boy who disappeared quickly and reappeared at a run with a cup of tea for me.

In the meantime, Waled chatted amiably with the men. I didn't see any weapons and had I not known better, I would have thought this a typical market and social center for the city's retirees. But this was the weapons black market. Weapons sale was strictly illegal here, but the authorities looked the other way. Corruption was common in the Kurdish Region, and if you had money, as the arms dealers did, you could get away with anything.

Waled eventually returned with a man who discreetly showed me an M16 from his nearby car. It was old, probably donated or sold to the Iraqi army by the Americans sometime after seeing service in the 2003 invasion. I asked for a price.

"He wants $2,200 for it. It's a good price," Waled said.

It was   actually a stiff price, but in a seller's market I went for it. I also bought a brand-new Glock 19 pistol, a shorter version of the Glock 17 I had used back home. At $3,100 it was almost four times more expensive than in Norway, but even though there were cheaper used pistols available, I wanted a reliable, familiar one. A pistol is the best insurance against being taken alive by the enemy. A well-placed bullet to my temple was my exit plan. It was crucial there would be no malfunctions while firing, which often happened with cheaper pistols.

I also bought extra magazines and ammunition and an optical sight for the rifle. At the end of the day, I had spent more than $6,000. We left the market and drove to a liquor store, where Waled bought a small bottle of vodka before heading back to the front. We drove in one of the general's SUVs, equipped with blue emergency lights that Waled used relentlessly as he screamed along at ninety miles per hour, the emptying bottle of vodka in his lap. He stopped to take a piss and chew gum. He said he couldn't sleep at the front without being a little drunk and hoped I wouldn't tell anyone. I was thoroughly unimpressed.

Back in Baqofah I now felt ready for life at the front. I had personal weapons and had taken on responsibility for one of the squad weapons. The Peshmerga mainly used Soviet-produced arms, so our arsenal consisted of PKM machine guns, RPG-7 rocket-propelled grenade launchers, and .50 caliber and 14mm heavy machine guns. I was surprised to find a German MG1 machine gun, a predecessor to the MG3 I had used in Afghanistan. The gun had belonged to an ISIS commander the general had killed in Sinjar, and no one knew how to operate it. There were no protests when I claimed it and laid it under my bed. In a bag I'd take to the front line I put four hundred rounds for the machine gun, extra ammunition for the rifle, the GPS, caffeine pills, water and a field ration, everything I'd need for at least twenty-four hours.

Over the coming weeks I spent most of my time in the village, but we rushed to the front line periodically, sometimes because someone had seen the enemy sneak around in no man's land, or because we'd been notified an attack was imminent. Usually it was a false alarm, but sometimes the danger was real.

During one of my first nights on the front line we learned that ISIS was planning an attack. Both sides used unencrypted radio and the short distance between us allowed us to eavesdrop. ISIS often used code words, or let their foreign fighters do the talking; we overheard German, French and Russian. At other times, like this night, they didn't try to hide their intentions, speaking Arabic, a language many Kurds understand. I was stationed with Roj and could hear the ISIS commander whisper orders to his men, who had made their way through the tall grass on the plain and settled in less than two hundred yards from the front line. It was pitch black and completely silent. We couldn't see anything, but we knew they were out there somewhere.

The ISIS fighters reported they could see the infidels, us, and their commander told them to prepare to open fire. My heart pounded. Then came the command. "Allahu Akbar" rang over the radio, repeatedly. The hairs on the back of my neck stood up. I switched off my safety. This was what I had come for. I would finally meet the enemy face to face!

When the attack came on our right flank, more than a mile away, I could do nothing but watch the ensuing firefight until a coalition jet showed up. Only then did the enemy retreat.

Almost daily, ISIS fired a handful of mortar grenades or rockets from Batnaya. Usually they aimed for the front line, but at times they targeted our village. One day as I texted Susanne from our livingroom, a grenade struck outside our house. Stone shrapnel flew through the glass windows, hitting the brick wall next to me so hard chunks flew off.

I ran outside to find two disoriented soldiers crawling on the ground. They had been drinking tea in the garden when the grenade hit less than four yards away. A thick brick wall separating them from the grenade had saved their lives. We ran to the neighboring house, which was better protected. The cook put on tea and we waited in the living room as grenades rained down on the village.

A few months earlier the general's brother, Akram, was killed when a 120mm mortar grenade hit his position at the front line. Three others in his position had been severely injured. Although these attacks usually only led to material damage, it was just a matter of time before ISIS again would get lucky.

ISIS had good logistical support and enough grenades to fire at us every day. We did not. The few mortar grenades we had were saved for special occasions, which was very frustrating. On March 20, we celebrated Nouruz, an important holiday, and the general thought fireworks would be fitting. We set up an 82mm mortar on the front line and aimed it at Batnaya. The general made a short speech extolling the importance of our work: The local people trusted we would prevent the enemy from breaking through the front so they could carry out their normal lives and do things like celebrate Nouruz.

He then dropped a grenade in the mortar's muzzle and ran, ears covered. Silence. Our grenades were Chinese- and Iranian-made and of terrible quality. Nearly one-third malfunctioned, unthinkable back in Norway. A soldier carefully removed the grenade and the general tried again, this time with better luck. The grenade landed a few hundred yards away from the target, a warehouse where we often observed enemy activity. The general adjusted the angle of the tube and dropped another grenade. This one hit closer still. Adjustments continued until the grenades hit just next to the building.

It was a primitive way of using the mortar. Back in the mortar platoon we used advanced optical sights, GPS, laser-equipment, and computers to hit our targets. Here we used the "if God wants" principle. "If God wants us to hit the warehouse, we will hit the warehouse. If we miss, it was not meant to be." I knew that if we hit anything at all it would be pure luck and nothing else, but I still asked if I could drop some grenades.

The general let me take over. I knelt beside the mortar, dropped the first grenade down the tube, and hunkered down as low as possible to avoid the enormous pressure coming from the muzzle.

Two years earlier, a platoon colleague had lost a finger when his hand came too close to the muzzle during a live fire exercise at Rena. Another danger was so-called tube blast. Since Peshmerga grenades were of such poor quality and the tubes were poorly maintained, having an entire tube explode during firing wasn't unthinkable. In the '80s, three Norwegian soldiers died in such an accident. If it could happen in Norway, it could definitely happen here. It would at least be a quick and painless death, I told myself.

I shot a handful of grenades, and the guys were impressed with my technique. Their practice was to run away as they dropped the grenade. They had never seen anyone kneel calmly next to the tube during firing. Thereafter, I was often asked to help set up and man the mortar.

ISIS responded to our attack with their own grenades and a 23mm machine cannon. I lay in one of the positions on the berm as cannon projectiles flew right overhead. "Swish, swish, swish." I was experiencing direct fire for the first time in my life. I was underwhelmed. The distance between us and the enemy was too great, and I had good cover in my position, which made me feel like I wasn't in real in danger. I hoped ISIS would launch a direct attack at our front, not knowing my wish would be fulfilled soon.

In the early morning gray, I jolted awake to a barrage of incoming grenades. We usually slept through such interruptions, but this time I suspected something significant. I was climbing out of my sleeping bag when a soldier on guard shoved the door open and sounded the alarm. In few minutes I was fully dressed and in the street with my rifle, my bag on my back, the machine gun on one shoulder and a box of extra ammunition in the other hand.

The general shouted commands to soldiers readying the vehicles and squad weapons. He ordered me into one of the pickups. I threw myself into the back as the driver put the pedal to the floor and almost lost me. We turned onto the road to the front line, a long, straight stretch, and the driver slowed down. Ahead we could see the grenades' impact.

The driver hesitated. I banged on the rooftop repeatedly, shouting "Go, go, go!" He sped toward the house on the front line, which was under heavy attack. Just before we arrived, a grenade struck right in front of us. Earth and pebbles flew high in the air. It was just like the movies!

I charged into the house, up the stairs, onto the roof, into position and readied the machine gun. The soldiers on duty told me to keep an eye on no man's land; a direct attack often followed such a bombardment. Grenades rained down and one struck right next to the house.

"Lucky," I thought, not knowing a soldier on the first floor had been injured by the shrapnel. After an hour and a half, the attack subsided. Birds chirped as though nothing had happened.

Just a few hundred yards down on our left flank, an intense firefight erupted in another unit's position. An unknown number of ISIS fighters hidden in the grass had opened fire on our soldiers, who fought back with everything they had. I monitored our sector, but it was clear the attack was focused on our neighbors. The general and a handful of men from our Quick Reaction Force provided support on the flank. The shooting stopped, and I spotted a group of our soldiers moving towards the trench to investigate, a move that proved fatal.

One Peshmerga soldier was shot in the head and died instantly. Another grabbed his buddy's motionless body and dragged him back to the berm under covering fire.

"There! There! Daesh!" men on the roof shouted. I looked back as eight or ten ISIS fighters emerged from the tall grass by the neighboring town. They were out of our range and they knew it. Taunting us, they calmly walked in a straight line to the road to Batnaya and disappeared into the town. Their mission was complete.

I left the guard post in the afternoon and met Saad, who had been with the general during the attack.

"Where were you, Mike?" he asked. "You should have been with us on the flank. We killed two suicide bombers and look what I found on one of them!" He grinned as he proudly showed off a captured knife. "Come on, let's go get a look at them."

The media were already there. A local TV station's female journalist reported from in front of the bodies with a semicircle of soldiers standing around her. When she finished, two of her colleagues took selfies with the bodies in the background. It was the first time I had seen corpses in real life. I was surprised at how waxy they looked.

The suicide bombers had used the firefight's chaos to scale our trench with a ladder. They had run toward the berm but were stopped by a hail of bullets before they could jump into our positions and blow themselves up. One looked local, the other Western with a clean-shaven face and long, dark blonde hair. He was handsome and would have been popular with the ladies if it weren't for the bullet holes and the piss on his pants. Flies were gathering, especially on the local guy, who was shot in the face and had one arm nearly shot clean off. I took a couple of pictures with my phone and walked back to the truck. I had had my first taste of battle.

8 POWER OF THE MEDIA

One of the first things I did when I arrived in Baqofah was to create a new Instagram account to document my experience. I had Internet through Fastlink, a wallet-sized mobile router I bought in Duhok. Fastlink provided a wireless network around me and I could download data at broadband speeds, an impressive feat considering the country's terrible infrastructure. I had no clear goals for my Instagram account, only a thought that I was about to do something out of the ordinary that should be documented.

My first posts were quite innocent, just routine photos of life at the front. I blurred out my face and other details that might reveal my identity and nationality, not because I feared the Norwegian government would figure out where I was - I expected that to happen eventually - but because the Telemark Battalion was about to deploy to Northern Iraq. I saw no reason to create problems for anyone back home.

My account gained followers quickly and it didn't take long for the guys at Rena to start following me. The inevitable had happened, but I never imagined the consequences.

A few days later I received a text message from Dilshad, who had talked to Eivind. My entire squadron had been summoned to the Camp Rena auditorium, where an officer revealed where I was, what I was doing and said my actions were completely illegal because I was still technically employed by the Army. He said the Peshmerga was guilty of war crimes, a crazy statement considering the Telemark Battalion trained them.

He went on to say the battalion had notified the Norwegian Police Security Service and that I would be prosecuted when I got home. Anyone caught following me on Instagram or having any contact with me risked losing their jobs.

I had known leadership wouldn't welcome my decision, but would I really be prosecuted? Their reaction hit me hard. Did others in my battalion consider me a traitor who had abandoned them and gone down on my own? Or did they understand my choice? I couldn't tell.

Communication from Rena stopped completely after Dilshad's text. It hurt that my former brothers in arms cut me off, even though I understood the power of leadership's threats. Some I considered friends blocked me on other social media sites too. Leadership had done a good job scaring them away.

Social media revealed what others in Norway's armed forces thought. In a private message shown to me by a friend, the Cadet Society, the Norwegian Military Academy's student society, had labeled me a mercenary. Was this view shared by more in the forces, or was it only an ignorant few? I was a volunteer, here at my own expense, fighting for what I believed! I decided to focus on my job in Iraq and keep chronicling my daily life on Instagram.

On April 1, my employment with the military officially ended. My final paycheck was due that day, a large sum I was depending on for my continued volunteer service. I had already spent more than $12,000 on transport, equipment, weapons and other expenses at the front. Because of the economic crisis, many Peshmerga didn't even receive their wages; sad, but admirable. Soldiers would spend a week risking their lives at the front, then spend their week off at home working a second job to support their families. As I was slightly better off than local Peshmerga, I often bought food and drink for my team at a nearby village. At times I bought fuel for our vehicles, always scarce across the entire front.

I was counting on my final paycheck for future ammunition purchases. When payment didn't arrive, I knew something was really wrong. I tried contacting my squadron leadership to learn if they were holding my money back or if it was a simple mistake. I never got a response. It seemed they were forcing me to fail and return to Norway with my tail between my legs.

I contacted a renowned lawyer in Oslo who had defended many Norwegian Islamists, including foreign fighters for ISIS. Although he represented the same people I hoped to face on the battlefield, I knew he found ISIS' actions as abhorrent as I did.

We agreed I should cease contact with squadron leadership. He would contact the Norwegian armed forces and PST on my behalf to secure my final payment and eliminate the possibility of prosecution. They ignored him, too.

He told me about a journalist friend at the Norwegian newspaper Dagbladet, who might be interested in telling my story. Media attention would force the battalion to answer. I had to think about it. I had planned to stay away from the media. I wanted to avoid problems for the Rena force headed to Erbil that revealing my nationality publicly might create. But what choice did I have? The military was holding my paycheck hostage and refused to communicate. One would think I'd joined ISIS. I felt pushed into a corner.

"Let's do it. Let's go," I told the lawyer after a couple of days.

At the end of April, I asked the general for a few days off. Dagbladet was sending the journalist and a photographer, but they didn't want to come to the front. We agreed to meet in Erbil. I had been at the front for nearly two months straight, had lost a lot of weight from our inadequate diet and had a big sleep deficit. The general thought I could benefit from getting away for a bit and gave me a week off. For the first time since I arrived in Baqofah, I put on civilian clothes and got in a cab for Erbil.

I checked into my old hotel, this time with greater confidence. I was no longer scared of being kidnapped, but still slept with the pistol under my pillow, a habit I had developed at the front. The journalist stayed at Erbil Rotana, one of the city's most expensive hotels with nightly room rates equal to an average Kurd's monthly salary. After a thorough pat down and temporary confiscation of my folding knife, the guards outside the hotel waved me into the premises.

The contrast with where I'd spent the last two months stunned me. The place was opulent. Most guests appeared to be Western journalists, aid workers, businessmen and diplomats. Dagbladet paid for lunch in the restaurant; it was the best meal I'd had in a long time. Over the next two days I was interviewed, photographed and filmed. Both the journalist and the photographer seemed genuinely sympathetic to my cause and I hoped this view would be shared back home. The next couple of days I spent mostly in my Ankawa hotel room, where I took showers and slept in, a luxury I didn't have at the front.

Back in Baqofah, I eagerly awaited the story's publication. A few days later I appeared on the front page of Dagbladet, anonymized and under the headline "I won't hesitate to kill." The headline irritated me. The quote had been my answer to "What do you do if an ISIS fighter is about to shoot you?" Despite the tabloid angle, it was a good story and solved many of my problems.

Dagbladet had contacted the armed forces and PST and, although the military denied having held my final payment, it was clear they lied. The money was deposited in my account the day the story hit. To my great relief, PST also said they weren't interested in prosecuting me. It was now clear to everyone that I hadn't broken the law and that Telemark Battalion leadership had vengefully overreacted.

Then and there I realized the power of the media and how I could use it. By gaining a following and making myself relevant, it would be harder for Norwegian authorities to undermine me and I could remain at the front. Soon, both Norwegian and foreign press regularly interviewed me, probably to the annoyance of those back home who wished I would keep a low profile.

I found incredible support on Instagram, where I now had several thousand followers all over the world. It touched me that so many people cared about the conflict and, like me, had been provoked by ISIS' horrific actions. Earlier, I had felt I was fighting alone. But daily messages in my inbox showed that many people wanted to contribute through encouraging words, care packages and financial aid. It gave me hope.

I received many inquiries from Westerners wanting to fight at the front. Most were not serious or unqualified, but a few were veterans with experience in both Afghanistan and Iraq. Most Peshmerga units, including my own, didn't accept foreigners, so I politely declined all physical support and referred people to the few units I knew could take them.

My goal from the start had been to participate in Mosul's liberation. I had imagined the offensive would start sometime in 2015 and last a couple of months. But in mid-May, to everyone's surprise, ISIS captured the large Iraqi city of Ramadi. By driving out Iraqi forces, ISIS proved it could still conquer new and critical areas despite being bombed daily. It was a big setback for the Iraqis, the American-led Coalition and for us in the north. I realized the Mosul offensive would be postponed indefinitely, and I would have to stay at the front longer than planned. My finances were running dangerously low. Again, I turned to social media.

Through online "crowdfunding," individuals or organizations present projects in need of financing, ranging from small business establishment, to art projects, to political campaigns and charitable causes. Donors contribute any amount, the theory being that if many contribute even small amounts, a large sum can result.

I had never heard of crowdfunding warfare, but I thought it was worth a shot. I set up a PayPal account and told my Instagram followers exactly what I needed. To my delight, many wanted to support my cause. Complete strangers sent money. Contributions were mostly small, but they allowed me to stay indefinitely and to support my unit with food, fuel and equipment. A few donors were very generous, like the Australian Afghanistan veteran who donated $1,000 out of nowhere. I withdrew the money from Duhok's only functioning ATM and over time bought binoculars, weapon parts and night optics for the frontline guard posts.

Since the beginning, I had been open and candid on Instagram about life at the front. Without exaggerating the situation or my abilities, I shared daily life and my opinions and views about the war in general. My honesty appealed to many and encouraged their support. But the support of those who mattered most was missing. There was still no word from Rena.

9 LIFE AT THE FRONT

During my nearly three months at the front, I had witnessed countless rocket bombardments and mortar shellings, but apart from the one battle in April, ISIS hadn't attacked us directly. The Coalition flew daily missions above us, keeping the Islamists on the defensive. Batnaya was regularly bombed and although this elicited cheers and raised spirits among the guys, I was afraid there would be no ISIS fighters left in the city when we went on the offensive.

Despite Coalition air support, we still took indirect fire daily. One day the general himself was struck in the forearm by shrapnel from a mortar grenade. An ambulance responded from the field hospital in Tel Skuf, and the driver sewed the wound shut in the field without anesthesia. The general showed no sign of pain and cursed ISIS as cowards for not daring to meet us face to face. I learned new swear words in Badini that day, and my respect for the general grew.

This was the general's fifth injury during the war against ISIS, testimony to how far forward he operated during battle. For Westerners, it is unthinkable for a general to put himself in as much danger as Wahed did. But this was the norm among Kurds. Leaders were expected to be present. To maintain morale among his soldiers he had to lead from the very front. In a unit that received no salary, had barely any resources and was exposed to almost daily attacks, his presence was critical.

Despite the general's popularity, many chose to leave the unit that summer. Conditions had become unbearable even for the tough and persistent Kurds. New soldiers joined us, usually young and without military training or experience. They were handed a rifle and three magazines and sent straight to the front. Uniforms and everything else they had to buy themselves, even ammunition. Some weren't even issued their own rifle and were reliant on finding a squad weapon they could man if a firefight broke out. I was embarrassed to recall my time in the armed forces when we complained the leather gloves we were issued weren't good enough, field rations weren't tasty enough and that the base store lacked shoeshine.

Even with a steady flow of new soldiers, the unit shrank. Many men I had gotten to know during the spring disappeared, including Ghasem, the Swedish cook. The new cook, Dara, was flamboyantly effeminate in body language and tone of voice. Any doubt I had about his sexual orientation disappeared the day he came on to me. He told me he had grown up outside Bagdad and just after the invasion in 2003 had acquired an American soldier friend with whom he traded what he discreetly referred to as "a massage." He wondered if I was interested in the same. I explained that I had a girlfriend back home in Norway, and politely declined his offer, to his obvious disappointment. The guys in the unit had a surprisingly relaxed attitude toward Dara. It wasn't unusual to walk into the TV room and find three guys dry-humping him to an amused audience. It was like being back at Rena.

I was tired of waiting. Tired of being shelled day after day without the ammunition to retaliate. I was less than nineteen miles from Mosul and knowing what the civilians were undergoing without being able to do anything about it was agonizing. Horror stories abounded about ISIS' treatment of the inhabitants, Muslim and non-Muslim. Homosexuals were thrown from rooftops, women were stoned to death for alleged infidelity, and young women and children were sold like cattle between Islamists. Girls as young as nine were pregnant after being held as sex slaves. My desire to help these people was unquenchable even though I had been in the country for so long.

I considered joining another unit, but after some research, discovered the situation was largely the same across Iraq's entire Kurdish front. The Peshmerga were supposed to hold the line until the Kurdish government and the Coalition launched the offensive. No one knew when that would happen, especially not after Ramadi fell.

I had imagined combat would be much more dynamic, but everyday life at the front was often monotonous. There was nothing to do but be patient and hope offensive operations wouldn't be delayed much longer. To make time pass, I trained with a rusty barbell and some old weight plates I found in an abandoned home. It was hard to train in my undernourished state, but it felt good to challenge my body a little. Physical exercise had always had a therapeutic effect on me.

One evening while out running, I heard whimpering from a cemetery on the outskirts of the village. The cemetery was surrounded by a tall wall with a single gate; the interior was overgrown with grass and brush. I went inside but saw nothing through the vegetation. I whistled and from under the bushes seven small puppies came running excitedly toward me. I was probably the first person they had ever seen. It was a sweet moment. I played with them for a while, and that evening Susanne and I talked about rescuing them. I hesitated, not sure the puppies would survive without their mother. Susanne told me to try my best. If they died, at least they would have experienced the love of a human being.

The next day I awoke to a grass fire raging on the village outskirts. I got up on the roof in time to see it jump the cemetery wall and engulf the interior. I deeply regretted having visited the night before, knowing now what was trapped inside. As soon as the fire died down I raced to the cemetery. Under one of the tombs I found a den and to my delight, all the puppies were alive. From that day forward, I regularly brought them food and water and they became my friends.

I spent my nights at the front line, either on the roof on guard duty or in one of the positions below. Since we were short staffed I volunteered for extra shifts, which the guys appreciated. Every evening I put on my uniform, packed my bag, and headed to the waiting pickup truck with the MG1 machine gun on my shoulder. At the front line I found my assignment, usually with two or three other soldiers, set up the machine gun with the rifle next to it, readied the ammunition and swallowed a caffeine pill or two, usually with a Wild Tiger. Then I waited 'til sunrise when the pickup truck returned for me.

American special forces often visited our front. They dressed in civilian clothes and drove armored SUVs, which could easily be mistaken for ordinary cars. They kept a low profile because of President Obama's promise not to involve American ground troops in the war. American special forces didn't participate in direct battles against ISIS, although this would change. At the time, they mostly sent up surveillance drones, gathered intelligence, and led aircraft to their targets.

"Can't you bomb the water tower in Batnaya for us?" I asked during a meeting with the Americans and the general. "Daesh uses it to observe and correct their indirect fire, and they're getting very accurate." It was only a matter of time before they hit the bullseye. "They also use the village church for meetings. We often observe activity there."

Unfortunately, the Americans' strict rules of engagement forbid bombing critical infrastructure and religious buildings without special permission from Erbil or Bagdad. The general was visibly upset.

"Half the town is in ruins, what difference does a single water tower make?" he asked. "We are Muslim, but in Sinjar we blew up a mosque Deash used to shoot at us. It's only a building. It can be rebuilt." The Americans nodded. They seemed as frustrated as we were.

I had a hard time understanding why the Coalition didn't do more to defeat ISIS militarily. Conspiracy theories abounded about how the West had secretly built up - and now supported - ISIS. When the West didn't do everything in its power to destroy ISIS, it was understandably that these theories prevailed among the poorly educated populace.

Many Coalition nations, including Norway, focused instead on training the local forces to fight ISIS themselves. In Norway, some argued this was more than enough, asserting that Middle East conflicts didn't concern us. But the migration crisis and ISIS attacks in Europe would soon prove ISIS a global problem. We had a moral imperative to destroy ISIS by any means necessary.

After several delays, Norwegian forces finally arrived in Erbil. The armed forces were secretive about the mission, but through Instagram I had befriended a few Coalition soldiers who shared information about the Norwegians. The Norwegian section in the international camp in Erbil, wasn't ready in time for their arrival. The solution was to check the entire force into Divan Erbil, the most expensive hotel in town, even more luxurious than the Erbil Rotana. With armed guards, restaurants, bars, swimming pools and everything else, room prices start at several hundred dollars per night. The first contingent spent four months at Divan Erbil. Later that fall the news got out in Norway.

"Norwegian soldiers in Iraq stayed in a luxury hotel," and "Armed force spends $3 million on a hotel" on the front page of Norwegian papers must have been very embarrassing for the military.

Norway wasn't the only country to billet its soldiers in hotels while waiting for space in the international camp. But other nations chose cheaper hotels that still provided reasonable security. Norway's expensive choice was odd, but I wasn't surprised. I was well acquainted with waste from my time in the armed forces. Three million dollars could have achieved a lot at the front, I thought.

The war in Syria and Iraq attracted many Western citizens who wanted to fight ISIS. Most joined the Kurdish YPG militia in Syria, which actively recruited foreigners through Facebook. YPG had few enlistment requirements, so numerous applicants without military experience were accepted. When war broke out in Northern Iraq, many Westerners joined the Peshmerga, but this was frowned upon by the Coalition. Some Western nations condemned their citizens who fought ISIS on their own terms while their governments balked at contributing boots on the ground.

Rumor had it that America and Canada had pushed the Kurdish government to forbid the Peshmerga from accepting foreigners into its ranks. To some extent they succeeded. Western volunteers were stationed far from the fighting out of fear they would be killed or captured by ISIS.

Most Westerners who found their way to Northern Iraq were placed in the 9th Brigade outside Kirkuk. Since Western foreign fighters attracted international press, the brigade welcomed them. The officers could promote themselves, their units and the Kurdish cause to an international audience, usually in that order.

Many volunteers saw through the charade and left in short order. Others embraced the hero status this afforded them at home and stayed for longer, even though they weren't allowed in combat. This was especially true for Westerners with a troubled past. The Kurds didn't run background checks on foreigners, so many saw the Peshmerga as an escape from their problems. Debt slaves, former criminals, wanted rapists and scammers found their way to the Peshmerga. Only after several unfortunate episodes in the fall of 2016 did this practice finally end.

The Assyrian militia in Duhok also accepted foreigners. Dwekh Nawsha, "those who sacrifice" in Syriac, was formed in the summer of 2014 to defend the Assyrian population from ISIS. As Christians, Assyrians were particularly vulnerable to the Islamists' ravages. Dwekh Nawsha consisted of just forty soldiers with no military training. The unit was purely symbolic but received substantial financing from Christians abroad. It used the same media strategy as the 9th Brigade.

Early in 2015, several Westerners were recruited into Dwekh Nawsha through Facebook. They were housed in Duhok and told they'd be sent to the front if they promoted the group on social media and talked to foreign press. After several months in Duhok, many left in frustration. Dwekh Nawsha leadership eventually agreed to send the remaining Westerners to the Kurdish front. Our front.

Dwekh Nawsha occupied the third inhabited house on our block in Baqofah. A few soldiers lived there but never appeared at the front line. I guessed it was important for the group's promotion and fundraising efforts to claim a presence at the front, but many of the Assyrians seemed uncomfortable so close to the action. So, it was a happy day in late May when a handful of Western Dwekh Nawsha volunteers turned up and showed an interest in supporting us. I took two of our new neighbors to inspect the front line.

British Jim was fifty-three and already a grandfather. His head was shaved and his arms covered in tattoos. He looked hardcore but struck me as nice guy. He loved talking about his dachshunds back home in England and gladly showed me pictures on his phone. Jim had no military experience, but Louis, from Texas, did.

Louis was in his mid-twenties and had seen combat in Afghanistan with the United States Marine Corps. He seemed professional, albeit somewhat overeager at times, was energetic, talked constantly and was full of new, creative ideas on how we could hurt the Islamists in the neighboring town. His ideas were impractical, but proved his dedication to the cause, which I respected. Perhaps most important was that Louis was a team player. Many volunteers had big egos, which often led to internal conflict. Louis, on the other hand, was humble. He was there to support the locals in their war against ISIS, not to make a name for himself.

I brought Jim and Louis up on the berm and pointed out areas of particular interest. In front of us, two white pillars of smoke rose suddenly from Batnaya.

"They're sending up rockets. Let's go up on the roof. It's safer there and we'll have a better vantage point," I told them calmly. We were almost to the house when two rockets struck in no man's land just a few hundred yards behind us. I turned to look.

"They've probably seen us and will fire more rockets now. Welcome to the front, guys," I said with a grin.

We got to the roof as two more rockets shot up from the neighboring town. Unlike mortars, which you can hear for one or two seconds before impact, some rockets emit a shrill whistle for seven or eight seconds before they hit. Seven seconds is a long time to ponder imminent death.

The first two rockets landed so far away I wasn't terribly worried. I knew the next would hit closer. As suspected, the next two struck less than 350 yards from the house, still a comfortable distance. I checked my phone for new messages from Susanne. Jim and Louis kept calm through their first incoming fire since arriving at the front. Several more rockets hit no closer than a hundred yards from us before a jet screamed overhead and dropped a bomb over the rocket's launch site.

Louis thought he spotted movement in a building close to where the bomb hit and asked for permission to fire one of the PKM machine guns we had on the roof. The distance seemed outside the machine gun's practical range, but he had brought his own ammunition, so we let him fire a few bursts. Louis later told me he had developed post-traumatic stress disorder from his experiences in Afghanistan. He had feared a stress reaction when the first two rockets hit, but my calmness had had a contagious effect.

"A fucking good first day at the front," he said as he spit out a fat lump of chewing tobacco.

Back in Baqofah, the general gave me permission to bring Louis and the other Westerners to the front line when I went on guard duty. The Assyrians weren't happy. They feared the Westerners would decamp and join us, but they knew better than to oppose General Wahed. Jim wasn't interested in the front. He was happy staying in the village, where he was active on Facebook and often went back to the house in Duhok to rest.

"I came to support Dwekh Nawsha," he said. "Since Dwekh Nawsha isn't at the front line, I see no reason to take shifts there." He was honest, and I had no issues with his choice.

Louis and two Brits named James and Tim were more than willing to follow me. James had a deep, dark voice and a thick Scottish brogue that left no doubt as to his origins. He was a former soldier with experience in Northern Ireland. Although he was getting up in years, he was in surprisingly good shape.

Tim was also a good fit. The former bouncer, prison officer and craftsman had spent a good chunk of his life lifting weights and dreaming of being a soldier but had never passed the admission requirements for the British armed forces. Only now, at thirty-eight, had he realized his childhood dream by volunteering in Dwekh Nawsha. Different backgrounds aside, we four got along well and I was impressed by their professionalism. We spent many nights together at the front line.

One night, as rockets rained down on Louis, James and me, we heard one coming straight toward us. I curled up as small as possible and covered my head with my arms. Louis and James did the same. The rocket got louder and louder as it homed in. Our relief was palpable as it passed and landed far behind us.

"I almost shit my pants," Louis said. James and I burst out laughing. For outsiders I'm sure it's strange, but that's how it is; the relief of having survived, a self-defense mechanism. It's crucial to laugh in the face of danger or you won't last long. Sadly, Louis and Tim went home towards the end of the summer after much frustration with their treatment by the Assyrians and conflicts with other Western volunteers. But it wouldn't be the last time I saw them.

The Mosul offensive was delayed yet again as we waited for the Iraqis to reclaim the areas south of the city. Life at the front took its toll. More soldiers left the unit and logistics continued to deteriorate. At one point we had nothing to eat for four days but flatbread and old vegetables. I daydreamed about food and started planning my first order at McDonald's in Norway. In Afghanistan I had witnessed the locals living in poverty and hunger. Now I experienced it firsthand. It put things in perspective.

Sleep was another deprivation. Kurdish culture shows no consideration for sleeping people and Kurds have terrible sleep patterns. It wasn't unusual for the man in the neighboring bed to light up a cigarette at four in the morning and call a friend, talking as if he were alone in the room. Or for a group of soldiers to loudly argue about trifles next to a sleeping comrade.

We lacked power for fans much of the day, and sleep was next to impossible in the stifling heat after a long night shift. Next to my bed I kept a bottle I had poked a tiny hole in to sprinkle water over myself in an effort to stay cool. I often awoke to rats dashing across my bed, or the stinging bite of flies and other insects. Once I found a dead mouse under my sleeping bag. I had probably crushed it in my sleep.

Everything aside, the biggest hardship was being apart from Susanne.

Although we spoke daily, I had been gone for half a year and the war was becoming a major strain on our relationship. It was time to go home.

10 GOING HOME

Although I had spent far more time at the front than the rest of the unit, I felt bad leaving. Some Peshmerga troops had begun receiving paychecks, but we were not among them. The general often traveled to Erbil to negotiate pay and logistical support, with no luck. One of the older guys in the Quick Reaction Force considered selling one of his kidneys.

"I could get $2,000 on the black market," he said. "It's good money, about four months' pay."

The situation was desperate, especially since we knew huge amounts of oil money were disappearing into the pockets of corrupt politicians.

I asked Deldar, an officer in the Quick Reaction Force, to drive me to a nearby village to do some final shopping before going home. Deldar was in his mid-thirties and spoke fluent Sorani like Saad, which was why I had the strongest ties with the two. Even after six months, I struggled to understand the local dialect.

Hatarah was less than ten minutes away by car. The inhabitants were Yazidis, the religious minority most hated by ISIS. It wasn't often I visited nearby villages, mainly inhabited by Yazidis and Christian Assyrians, but every time I was reminded of the importance of our job at the front. Even if I hadn't experienced real combat, I had at least helped create some security for these people, living less than six miles from a brutal, reckless enemy bent on their eradication.

We parked at the bustling Hatarah market. It was hard to believe war was raging close by. A few weeks earlier, a false rumor that ISIS had attacked our front and driven us to retreat caused widespread panic in this and nearby villages. The inhabitants had fled for their lives towards Duhok and Erbil. I felt sorry for them, having to live under such conditions. At the same time, I knew they were among the lucky ones. More than a million Iraqis had been displaced internally by ISIS. At least the local villagers didn't

73

have to live in an overcrowded camp.

I bought eggs, bread, rice, vegetables, biscuits, soap, a couple cases of Wild Tiger and a live goat. I also bought a couple bags of powdered milk and asked Deldar to feed the village cats I was looking out for and keep an eye on the puppies in the cemetery while I was gone. On our way back, we stopped at a provisional gas station, a small shack where a boy no older than twelve sold fuel from old soda bottles and plastic containers. The fuel had obviously been diluted, as it was even in regular gas stations. The economic crisis had hit the country hard and people saved where they could.

I filled the tank and threw an extra container in the bed of the truck. Back in Baqofah spirits were high when we arrived with the food. Outside our house we slaughtered the goat the halal way, cutting the animal's throat and letting it bleed out. I wasn't a fan of this method, but it was the custom here. As a foreigner, I had to adapt my way of life, and not the other way around.

Deldar cut the throat while I helped hold the goat down. Blood poured out, as did the contents of the animals' bladder and bowel. Then Deldar showed me how to flay and butcher the animal and I gave him a helping hand. That evening we tasted meat for the first time in a week.

My plan was to spend two months in Norway, but I was prepared to take the first flight back to Northern Iraq if needed. I said goodbye to the boys in Baqofah and took a cab to Erbil. For the first time since meeting Dagbladet four months earlier, I slept in a clean bed, alone in a quiet room and ate proper food. I realized I should have gone home sooner. In the future, I had to get better at taking breaks from the war. I dropped my weapons, ammunition and equipment at a relative's place in Erbil and headed to the airport.

On August 29, half a year after I had left Norway, I was finally home. The transition from life at the front to life in safe Norway went surprisingly well. As I walked from Oslo Bus Terminal to Oslo Central Station early in the morning after a long bus ride from Stockholm, I was shrouded in anonymity, just another face in the crowd. Nothing distinguished me from the people headed to work.

The day before I left Erbil I had learned that seven Peshmerga soldiers had been killed when a mortar grenade struck one of our neighboring unit's positions. I knew it could just as well have been one of ours, with my friends and me in it. But I also knew better than to dwell on it. "What if?" is one reason many combat soldiers later develop psychological problems.

"What if that grenade had hit twenty yards to the right?"

"What if that roadside bomb had gone off as we drove over it?"

"What if I was hit by the sniper, and not the man next to me?"

I was determined not to think too much about my experiences at the front, but

rather, enjoy the time I got to spend at home.

My reunion with Susanne, which was what I had looked forward to the most, was better than I had imagined.

"You were worth the wait," she said after our first night together. She was simply amazing. How many would have gone through what she had for the last six months, and still put up with me? Our relationship had passed the test and I realized she was the one.

I met with the Norwegian Police Security Service, or PST, at its headquarters in Oslo shortly after I got home. I had been curious about the welcome I would get from the authorities. Would they still threaten me with prosecution? After a lengthy chat with two friendly and sympathetic PST employees, it was clear I hadn't done anything illegal and no one could prevent me from going back to my unit in Iraq. They even offered me a free follow-up with a psychologist, which I politely declined. I felt fine and saw no reason to waste the taxpayer's money.

PST weren't the only ones interested in talking to me. After I got home, I received a letter from the Defense Security Department, or FSA, which manages operative safety and preventive security measures in the Norwegian armed forces. It also administers all military security clearances. I had long assumed I'd lost my clearance after joining the Peshmerga, but the letter ignited hope that I might rejoin the military after I finished in Northern Iraq.

I was excited as I took the train to meet the FSA at Akershus Fortress in Oslo. Despite the Telemark Battalion's poor treatment, I still wanted to support Norway when it came to national security. I knew it was only a matter of time before Islamists struck Europe again. Oslo could be next.

For more than three hours I answered a barrage of questions in front of a video camera. I offered the FSA my full support in Iraq. Because I could travel relatively freely around the Kurdish Region and Norwegian forces couldn't, I volunteered to provide the military with accurate and timely intelligence. After all we had the same goal; defeating ISIS. Louis had provided intelligence for the Americans, and an Italian I would later know collaborated closely with Italian forces in Iraq. Presumably, other Western volunteers had similar deals with their respective countries.

The FSA seemed receptive and the agents promised an answer regarding my clearance before I returned to Iraq. As I left, one agent told me that my former colleagues from Rena had been at the fortress a few days earlier. The first contingent had just returned from Northern Iraq after a three-day stopover at a luxury hotel in Brussels. On their return, they had been escorted by police from Gardermoen military airport to the fortress for a medal ceremony with friends, family and leaders from the armed forces and the government. On my way out, I walked to the parade ground where my colleagues had proudly stood just a few days earlier. I paused and imagined how it would feel to be honored for my effort.

I enjoyed my time at home with friends and family and colleagues from the Telemark Battalion who were back in civilian life. Except for Eivind, I didn't see anyone still working at Rena. It appeared the embargo against me was still in effect. I met Eivind at a café in Oslo. It was good to see him again.

"So, how was your stay at Divan Erbil?" I laughed. Eivind explained what had transpired over the last four months. It was exactly as I had predicted. Training the Kurdish forces had been frustrating. The Kurds don't have a training culture like ours. Some would say they don't have a training culture at all, which I had experienced firsthand when I introduced the guys in Baqofah to simple combat techniques.

"It was like working in a kindergarten," Eivind said. "They kept finding excuses not to train. If it rained, they said that their guns would rust. Some of the soldiers even tried to beat up a general when they didn't get the weekend off. They may be tough in combat but training them is hopeless."

Even after that letdown, Eivind wanted to go back. He'd gotten to know some employees at a hospital in Sulaymaniyah, one of the Kurdish Region's larger cities, and had accepted a position as a volunteer emergency room nurse. He planned to leave the Telemark Battalion and go down in the new year. I was happy for him. Eivind lived for the medical profession, and in the emergency room he would get the experience he craved. The locals would benefit tremendously from his expertise.

Eventually Knut, a stranger who had messaged me on Instagram, joined us. He and a buddy were going to Syria, where they had been accepted into the YPG. Knut was a few years younger than me and had only his conscription as military experience. But he had recently worked with a private security company in Poland and had taken a weapons course on guns including the AK-47. Knut seemed calm and well-mannered; that he had flown from western Norway to meet me indicated his intentions were serious. Based on my knowledge of the situation in Syria, I told him what to expect from the YPG. Eivind and I took him to a military store to buy clothes and equipment for his coming trip. Before we went our separate ways, we agreed to stay in touch and try to meet up in Erbil one day.

I also met Karl Håkon, another stranger who had been inspired to join the Peshmerga when he read about me in Dagbladet. Karl Håkon was in his mid-twenties, tall, lanky, and sharp looking. He had been accepted into a Peshmerga unit outside Kirkuk through a Kurdish friend in Norway and would leave shortly. He had always dreamt of being a soldier but hadn't served his conscription, which made me wonder what he could contribute. At least he seemed genuinely engaged in the Kurdish cause.

I quickly learned the importance of having a network in Iraq. Every time I heard about new Western volunteers in the Kurdish Region, I contacted them through social media and milked them for information. I got a good overview of the volunteer community and the situation on the different fronts. In return, I helped them through my network of other volunteers, journalists, aid workers, and staff from private security firms. Many of the people I introduced developed long-term personal and professional relationships. One American dubbed me "The Godfather of Western volunteers."

After two months at home it was time to return to the war. Despite repeated inquiries, I had not heard back from the FSA. It was obvious they never intended to maintain my security clearance. I felt tricked and cursed my naivety for meeting them and answering all their questions. But I learned a lesson: I couldn't trust the armed forces. They had blown their chance to engage me for Norwegian intelligence. But why? Was I viewed as disloyal? Although I had replaced the Norwegian flag on my uniform with the Kurdish one, my loyalty remained first and foremost with Norway. This was where I had grown up, where I had my life.

I wasn't the only one the armed forces was gunning for. A young man in a Home Guard Task Force contacted me on Instagram saying he had been picked up by military police during a field exercise and led to a barracks basement, where intelligence officers interrogated him roughly and made insane accusation; his beard supposed proof he wanted to be a foreign fighter. Why? He had left a comment on one of my Instagram posts, an innocent statement of support for my work.

I couldn't believe Norwegian intelligence could be so unprofessional, or that they had nothing better to do than harass their own soldiers. The young man lost his clearance and his job on the spot and military police escorted him home to relinquish his gear in front of his shocked family. He was a scapegoat intended to scare others from contacting me or showing support. Freedom of expression was apparently not as protected in the forces as in the rest of Norwegian society and I began to understand why my former colleagues from Rena had severed contact. Still, I will always be willing to go to war and give my life for Norway.

I said goodbye to my family, who still weren't fully aware of my activities in Iraq. I had told my parents I was stationed in Tel Skuf with an existing group of Western volunteers who trained local forces, and that I was out of danger. I knew they wouldn't deal well with the thought of me on the front line and I hoped to save them more sleepless nights with this lie.

A few months earlier I feared my mother had learned the truth as I spoke with her on the phone outside our house in Baqofah. A grenade whizzed over me and I had time only to throw myself on the ground before it struck behind the house with a loud bang. Amazingly, my mother didn't hear the explosion. I continued the conversation as if nothing had happened, with my heart in my throat and my pulse racing.

The hardest part was saying goodbye to Susanne. We spent our last day together in Oslo ending with dinner at a restaurant. The mood was somber and neither of us said a word as we walked towards Oslo Central Station for our final goodbye, my arms around her.

"Why do you have to leave?" she asked when we reached the platform. I no longer had a good answer. I could come up with nothing to justify what I had put her through for the last six months, or for leaving again.

"I just have to, Sweetie," I said. She buried her face against my chest, and I smelled her hair. We stood like this into the night. I felt her warm breath and tears moistening my shirt. I was going to miss her more than anything else.

"Why do you have to go?" She whispered again.

11 THE BATTLE OF SINJAR

Back in Erbil I retrieved my equipment from my relative and checked into a hotel in the center of town. The receptionist seemed skeptical of my luggage.

"Do you have any weapons?" he asked, pointing to the "no guns" sign behind the counter.

"No, no weapons here," I answered politely. An ever so little lie. In my room I took out my rifle and pistol. I had cleaned them before going home, but I could leave nothing to chance. One cleaning too many was better than one too few. I cleaned the weapons again, brushed off every single bullet - almost five hundred in total - changed batteries in the electronic equipment, and examined the rest of my gear and clothing.

I mounted the new rifle parts an Israeli company had donated against a promise to promote their products on Instagram. After the upgrade, the rifle no longer looked like a relic from the Vietnam War. I was constantly contacted by companies that wanted to see their products used in the war against ISIS, but I never promoted products I didn't intend to use.

Before arranging transport back to the front, I visited the civilization museum across from my hotel. That fall, Susanne and I had visited many of Oslo's museums, although she wasn't as enthusiastic as I was. The museum in Erbil featured several antique sculptures as well as ancient jars, stone tablets and other objects of marble, pottery and bronze. In one hall, a group of young Italian archeology students circled a large table brushing sand and dust from objects that seemed to have come straight from the field.

This region was rife with history: Alexander the Great, the Mongols, the Romans had all been here and left their mark. I tried to imagine the 311 BC Battle of Gaugamela in today's Mosul, when outnumbered Macedonians and Greeks defeated the Persian Goliath and changed the course of history. Tens of thousands died in that encounter. The coming battle of Mosul would be at least as bloody. History repeats itself, especially in this part of the world.

Back in Baqofah, I discovered that the general and half the Quick Reaction Force had left for Sinjar a few days earlier. There had long been talk of a coming offensive to retake the city from ISIS, and the assault was about to kick off. An officer called the general to say I was back and wanted to join the offensive. I held my breath awaiting his answer.

"Okay, so a car is coming to take you to Sinjar tonight," the officer said. "Two others from the Quick Reaction Force will go with you. Bring only a backpack." I started packing immediately. A teammate came into my room and handed me a shoulder patch for my uniform.

"It's new. Everyone in the unit has to wear it," he said. I looked at it and smiled. Our new symbol was a skull inspired by the comic character The Punisher, the same character that caused the 2010 Telemark Battalion media outrage and accusations of a festering subculture. The irony wasn't lost on me.

Adrenaline rushed through me, as it had at the hotel in Erbil eight months earlier when Agit told me I was going to Sinjar. My hands shook, and my mouth got dry. We were finally attacking the enemy!

Early the next morning the driver showed up several hours late. His car, an old Opel, was a complete wreck and I predicted it would break down before we reached Sinjar. Ahmed, Bakhtiar and I said farewell to the team and climbed into our dubious transport. Adel, our other cook, gave us a hug and burst into tears.

"Take care of yourselves," he cried. It was serious now.

On June 29, 2014 ISIS had independently declared a Muslim state, or "caliphate," in Syria and Iraq, with Iraqi Abu Bakr al-Baghdadi as its supreme leader. At the time, ISIS controlled vast areas of the two countries. Conquering Mosul had made the terror group very rich. When ISIS fighters took the city in June without resistance from fleeing Iraqi forces, they seized more than $400 million in cash from the central bank in Mosul. In addition, ISIS earned millions of dollars daily by selling oil, gas and looted treasures to local and foreign traders. Mosul also served up huge caches of surplus military material left by the well-equipped Iraqi army. Almost overnight, ISIS went from a ragtag terror group to a terror state unlike any the world had ever seen.

Abu Bakr al-Baghdadi was a man of great ambitions. One month after claiming its caliphate, ISIS began its offensive in Northern Iraq. Several cities fell to the Islamists, including Sinjar, not far from the Syrian border. Sinjar's inhabitants were mainly Yazidis, their religion closely related to Zoroastrianism, an ancient tradition tracing its origins to today's Iran. On August 3, ISIS fighters moved into Sinjar and nearby villages from the south, forcing more than fifty thousand Yazidis to flee up the Sinjar Mountains just north of the town.

Those who didn't escape suffered a terrible fate. More than five thousand boys and men were executed on the spot. Nearly seven thousand women and children were taken as slaves. Of those who managed to flee, many perished in the following days from extreme heat, thirst and starvation. ISIS laid siege to the mountains. Fear that terrorist forces would advance up the mountains to continue their genocide against the Yazidis prompted American airstrikes against ISIS around Sinjar on August 9.

Because Sinjar had been an important reason for my joining the Peshmerga, the promise of taking part in its liberation was exhilarating. As the old Opel chugged up the Sinjar Mountains, I just hoped we weren't too late.

The checkpoints we passed through were controlled by the Kurdish PKK, a military and political organization whose ideology is based on Marxism-Leninism. Since the mid '80s, the group has engaged in armed conflict in Turkey in response to the Turkish state's oppression of the Kurds. Many of their assaults hit civilian targets as well as military ones. For that reason, some consider the PKK a terrorist organization.

The PKK had nevertheless proved to be very effective in the war against ISIS. PKK guerillas, along with American airstrikes, played a key role in breaking the siege of the Sinjar Mountains in August 2014. Many Yazidis saw the PKK as their saviors and begrudged the Peshmerga, whose forces stationed in Sinjar had fled without taking up the fight against advancing Islamists. The relationship between the PKK and the Peshmerga under Masoud Barzani was tense after many years of conflict. How would they receive us, four Peshmerga traveling alone? Would they let us through? Would there be confrontation?

I decided not to resist if we were detained. Although I didn't agree with their ideology, I respected the PKK as warriors. I hadn't traveled down here to kill other Kurds, and I knew better than fucking with guerillas.

We reached the mountain's first checkpoint. The guard house was festooned with pictures of PKK's imprisoned leader, Abdullah Öcalan, and the organization's characteristic symbols and colors. We stopped the car and the guerillas examined us. To my relief we were waved through and cleared the remaining checkpoints without incident.

I was shocked to see several thousand refugees still living on the mountain under miserable conditions. Tents and provisional sheds lined the road. The inhabitants were burning garbage and scrap wood to stay warm and children walked barefoot in the cold mud. I hoped we could liberate

Sinjar quickly, so they could return to what was left of their homes. No one deserved to grow up under such conditions.

At the top of the mountain we stopped again for an Iraqi military helicopter that had landed in the middle of the road. Iraq supported the operation with medical evacuation and bomb disposal, two resources the Kurds lacked. I stretched my legs as we waited for the helicopter to take off.

From here I could see Sinjar at the foot of the mountain, surrounded by flat desert stretching to the horizon. It was easy to understand why the Yazidis had fled here; there was no place else to go. Large, black pillars of smoke rose beneath Coalition planes bombing the town. The smell of gunpowder from Kurdish artillery cannon on the mountain filled the air.

"They've been bombing the town for a full day now," Bakhtiar said.

"Are there no civilians left in the town?" I asked.

"No, only Daesh, so anyone we meet down there is considered hostile."

The helicopter finally took off and we got back in the car to begin the descent to Sinjar. For several hours, Kurdish offensive forces consisting of 7,500 women and men had streamed down Sinjar Mountain. At the base, the forces split in three to attack Sinjar from the west, north, and east. The area south of Sinjar was still controlled by ISIS. On our way down, we passed Peshmerga soldiers in trucks and old Soviet tanks, PKK and YPG guerillas in pickup trucks with mounted machine guns, Western special forces in civilian dress, Yazidi militia in minibuses and Kurdish special forces in newer American combat vehicles. Never had I seen such a large and varied assembly of military might.

Halfway down the mountain, the enormous column turned onto an old dirt track to avoid the many improvised bombs certain to lie along the main road. The terrain was demanding, and it didn't take long before the old Opel ground to a halt.

"I have to turn around. The car can't take any more," our driver said. "You'll have to walk from now on."

We tried calling the guys with the general, but the cellular network was overloaded, so we trudged down the mountain with our backpacks on and rifles in hand. Where the forces split at the foot of the mountain, we tried calling again, with no luck.

"Has anyone seen General Wahed Kovle?" Bakhtiar asked. Peshmerga soldiers posted at the intersection thought they had seen him drive south, so we continued straight ahead. The roadside was littered with countless bombs dug up and defused by the Iraqi bomb disposal squad. Many lives would have been lost without their help.

We passed vehicle after vehicle until we reached a group of Kurdish Special Forces dressed in black. We asked again about the general.

"He probably plans on attacking from the west or east. This is our northernmost forward vehicle, so your general can't have come through here," one said, pointing to a black armored combat vehicle just ahead. We had wasted nearly an hour walking down this road, and I started worrying we wouldn't find our guys at all.

We were about to turn around when shooting erupted behind nearby buildings. The fighting quickly intensified and several Special Forces soldiers jumped from their vehicles to assist. We threw off our backpacks to join them when the soldier we had spoken with told us to back down.

"We have the situation under control," he said, as bullets flew around us. We wanted to help but knew better than to interfere when we weren't wanted.

We trudged back to the intersection, where people swore they had seen the general drive both to the west and to the east. We decided to hedge our bets and wait at an established meeting point on the mountain. We started back up with arduous steps. Our backpacks were heavy, and I hadn't slept or eaten in more than a day.

Halfway up the mountain two hours later, Roj, the general's son, appeared in a pickup truck. He was a joyful sight. We threw ourselves into the back and proceeded west to a small village where the rest of the team waited.

Roj explained that when the offensive started that morning, our unit and a group of PKK guerillas had taken this village. They had killed a handful of ISIS fighters and an airstrike had leveled one of the houses. Our unit had established itself in another house and PKK had done the same. Kurdish forces had taken all the villages around Sinjar and our unit had captured two Islamists. They were guarded by female guerillas, which must have been humiliating given their medieval views of women.

Night was creeping in and we had to rest and set up a defense. The next morning, we would take Sinjar itself. I followed Roj and Haji, a Quick Reaction Force officer, to the bombed house. We searched the ruins. It was impossible to say exactly how many ISIS fighters had been inside. Limbs, chunks of flesh, bone shards and entrails lay scattered throughout, covered by a fine layer of sand, dust and flies.

"We got a lot of fire from this house when we approached the village, so we had the Americans bomb it," Haji said. He picked up a burnt-out combat vest and retrieved the magazines to see if any were usable. The magazines were smashed but much of the ammunition was fine. In addition, he found 50,000 dinars - about $40 - hidden in a magazine pocket. He was quite pleased.

Looting corpses is common and accepted by the locals. The rule is you can keep anything you find on a dead enemy except squad weapons, which go to your unit. Weapons, magazines, jewelry, watches, phones, wallets, and even shoes disappear before a corpse is cold.

About thirty yards from the house I glimpsed something I couldn't quite make out. I walked over for a closer look. It was the legs and groin of a dead ISIS fighter, his pants completely burned away. He had probably been on the roof when the house was bombed, launching him way over here. His torso was nowhere to be seen. Several corpses lay scattered around the village. The top of one Islamist's skull had been shot off, the contents gone. I had missed a good fight, and it annoyed me. I was comforted knowing there would be new opportunities the next day.

As one of the Yazidis' most important towns, Sinjar was symbolically key to ISIS and strategically vital, because it lay on the main road between Mosul and Raqqa, Syria. I would be surprised if ISIS didn't put up a fight, and I envisioned house to house combat in the coming days. Around midnight I went up to the roof to man our guard post. Earlier, ISIS had attacked the village with two suicide vehicles, but both had been shot to pieces by the general and the guys. We worried the Islamists would send more suicide bombers under the cover of night.

I had been awake since the previous morning, but I had no problem staying alert during my two-hour shift in the face of potential danger lurking in the dark. Sporadic shooting interrupted the night, with tracers streaking across the sky. Aircraft and artillery cannon on the mountain bombed the town mercilessly and sent shockwaves I felt through my entire body. It was a beautiful sight. I had an orchestra seat at this concert of death.

I awoke on the cold concrete floor. It was morning and we were attacking Sinjar! I had slept like a child, using my backpack as a pillow. Outside, the guys had prepared tea, freshly baked bread, honey and yogurt bought in a village on the other side of the mountains. The skies were blue and sunny but it was still chilly, so I kept my down jacket on for breakfast. The general was in high spirits after the previous day's fighting. He had personally killed several ISIS fighters by throwing hand grenades into houses.

After breakfast we geared up and I jumped into the bed of one of the pickups. We set off with the PKK along the main road to Sinjar in a long column of SUVs and pickups. We would attack from the west while other Kurdish forces would strike from the north and east. Nearing Sinjar, we jumped out of our pickup and continued on foot next to the slowly moving vehicles. An abandoned truck sat by the roadside. One of our guys raced over and tore the cover off the back.

"Out, get out!" he shouted in Arabic, pointing his rifle at a wounded ISIS fighter. The man jumped out quickly with his hands above his head and a crazed look in his eyes. He wore civilian clothes, his hair unkempt and large burns covered his face, chest and arms. The general questioned him on the spot.

The man didn't hide his affiliation with ISIS. He said he and two others had tried to escape west to Syria the night before but their car had been hit by a rocket, so they'd hidden in the truck overnight. The others had fled toward a nearby gas station when they saw us coming.

The general sent a team to find them, gave the prisoner water and sent him back to the village under guard for medical treatment. The man was burned black as coal and had suffered enough.

The guys returned from the gas station without prisoners and we continued toward town. I scanned the flat, barren landscape for cover in case we came under attack. We were sitting ducks; if anyone fired on us now we were in deep shit. It wasn't the best approach, but it was the Kurdish way to do things. I was surprisingly calm, but excited.

We got closer and closer to Sinjar without seeing any signs of life when someone spotted a car driving between buildings.

"Suicide vehicle!" he shouted. The general ran to his SUV, tore open the door and threw the driver out, ordering the rest of us to wait there. I immediately understood what he was doing and opened the passenger door, but he shouted at me to get out. My heart dropped as he slammed his door and drove toward the town at full speed.

The previous year, another renowned Peshmerga general had sacrificed his life to save his men by intentionally colliding with an advancing suicide vehicle. This general had received the honorable status of martyr, as did other Peshmerga who died in battle. Sometimes I thought Wahed also wanted to achieve martyrdom or be reunited with his brothers, all of whom had died in battle. Wahed could be reckless when it came to his own life. For those of us who loved him, it was hard to witness.

Just outside town, the general jumped out of his vehicle with a rocket launcher. We got ready as well, in case the vehicle got past the general. The car reappeared between buildings.

"Don't shoot, it's got the Kurdish flag on it!" someone shouted. It was one of our own who had taken the town from another direction.

The remaining Islamists had fled south during the night and we took Sinjar without resistance. The town was in ruins. I couldn't see a single intact building, and I thought about the refugees on the mountain. Was this what they would return to?

We walked into Sinjar; soldiers were firing guns in the air and waving flags, and local and international media swarmed in to report on the victory. Was it really over? Was this all? I felt bitter and disappointed that the enemy had deprived us of a good fight. I looked at the general. He seemed just as disappointed. The guys gathered around him in confusion.

"Get back in the cars. We're going south!" he barked.

Just outside town excavating machines were already digging a new front line against the enemy to the south. A soldier cautioned us that If we proceeded too far south, we risked getting bombed by the Coalition. Despite the warning, we continued into the desert.

After almost six miles we reached Qabusiye, a village which, at first glance, appeared abandoned. We searched the houses for ISIS fighters, but all we found were scared civilians. Qabusiye was inhabited by Muslim Kurds who feared the Yazidi militia had come to seek revenge. Although the Sinjar Region was populated primarily by Yazidis, it was also home to pockets of Arabs and Muslim Kurds. Some had been accused of collaborating with ISIS, and now they feared retribution.

The general assured the villagers they had nothing to fear from us or the Yazidi militia, and handed cigarettes to the men, who gladly accepted and told us the punishment for smoking under ISIS control was amputation of fingers.

Young and old approached us with tea, sweets, bread and yogurt. We were greeted as liberators and the atmosphere was relaxed. The general sent one of our men up a cell tower to fly the Kurdish flag; the villagers applauded.

Then the hunt for collaborators began. The villagers willingly showed us the homes of ISIS supporters. Although most had fled, we took three prisoners and a list of names Kurdish intelligence would find valuable. The prisoners, a father and his two sons, were led into separate rooms in an abandoned house at the outskirts of the village for questioning.

Deldar, Bakhtiar and I guarded one son, in his early twenties and nicely dressed compared to the other villagers. He was probably paid well by ISIS. Perhaps he had been involved in selling women, I thought, a lucrative trade. Now he leaned against the wall, blindfolded with his hands tied behind his back. Deldar did the questioning, and from what I could understand, the young man denied the charges. He didn't seem terribly worried, as he shook his head and sometimes laughed at Deldar's questions. That quickly changed when Raad entered the room.

Raad, an officer in our unit, was from Sinjar. Before the war he had earned good money as an interpreter for an American oil company. He had owned a big house, two cars and a large herd of sheep. He lost it all when ISIS occupied the town the previous year. Without a word, he started punching and kicking the prisoner. We dragged him away ; he switched off his rifle's safety and tried to aim at the prisoner, who had collapsed on the floor. Deldar and Bakhtiar had the situation under control, but I put on my hearing protection in case Raad fired. The room was small, and I didn't want tinnitus.

Deldar and Bakhtiar eventually took the rifle from Raad, who got out his knife and started hacking at the prisoner's beard. We let him cut a handful of hair before sending him out. Before the prisoner could get back on his feet, Saad came in and repeated the scenario. Saad had lost his home when ISIS captured Mosul, and he took it out on this guy. We eventually threw Saad out too, leaving the prisoner moaning on the floor. His grin was gone.

Back in Sinjar, the prisoners - including the bandaged ISIS fighter we had captured earlier - were displayed for local media. Kurdish intelligence took the prisoners, and we drove back to our house outside town. Of the seven hundred or so ISIS fighters who had occupied Sinjar, more than half had been killed the first day, most from the massive bombardment. The rest had fled, resulting in a total Kurdish victory. Although I should have been happy with the outcome, it was hard not to be disappointed about the short operation.

The following day we sat around a fire outside the house chatting and sipping tea; the atmosphere relaxed. We had been lucky to avoid any losses. The cellular network was working again, and I finally got to call Susanne. After I assured her the offensive was over and everyone was fine, she told me there had been a large ISIS attack in Paris the day before, with many fatalities. It was another grim reminder of why we must defeat this filth. Those at home might put the French flag across their Facebook profile pictures, but my fight against the Islamic State meant confronting terrorism on its home turf.

12 INTERNAL CONFLICTS

Back in Baqofah I reunited with James and Tim. Scottish James was one of Dwekh Nawsha's few remaining Western volunteers. Tim had gone home to England that summer but had quickly missed life at the front and returned to join a small group of mostly American and British volunteers based in Kirkuk. It would be one of very few Western groups to take part in offensive operations with the Peshmerga unit they supported. Tim's front had been quiet for a while, so he was spending a few weeks with us, hoping to find more action at our front.

It was good to see them again. I wished Louis had been there too. Jim, I learned, was gone. According to the others he had been ordered out of the country after buying cheap AK-47 rifles and selling them to Peshmerga soldiers for three times his cost. I took that report with a grain of salt; I knew James and Tim didn't get along with Jim.

Trash talking and rumors thrived among volunteers. Jim had created headlines back in the UK that fall, headlines the Norwegian press had caught wind of and reprinted. He was referred to as "The grandfather fighting ISIS" and claimed to have taken part in several heavy battles at our front. We had to laugh. What heavy battles was he talking about?

A few days after returning from Sinjar, we woke to yet another alarm in the middle of the night. By now I was used to waking abruptly. I dressed as fast as I could and ran to a waiting pickup truck with the MG1 machine gun, rifle and as much ammunition as I could carry. As we rolled past the neighboring house I saw James and Tim arguing with the Assyrians. They wanted to support us on the front line, which the Assyrians wouldn't allow. I realized it was just a matter of time before James would have had enough and leave. He might join another group where he could actually fight. No one could blame him. He had traveled all the way from Scotland to support his Christian brothers against ISIS, only to be used as a propaganda tool and source of income.

At the front line I raced to the roof and readied the machine gun, knocking down the bipod and placing it on the sandbags along the parapet. I checked the ammunition belt, opened the cover, inserted the belt and slammed the lid shut. I flipped up the front and rear sights and adjusted the rear sight to 1200 meters before loading and securing the weapon. Not only did I love the machine gun's rattle in operation, but I loved the sound of preparing it as well. It made me feel calm and safe, regardless of what was happening around me.

The general came up on the roof and said President Masoud Barzani had personally called to warn us about an upcoming attack. This is it, I thought. Fog crept silently over the front, engulfing us in just a few minutes. The street lights along the front line disappeared. If the enemy attacked now, we wouldn't see them before they were upon us. I adjusted the rear sight down to 200 meters, the shortest distance possible, and peered into the sea of fog. For all I knew, ISIS could already be crossing the trench with ladders and would open fire any second. I was ready, and my trigger finger was itching. Let them come so we can send them to Hell.

"What's that sound?" one of the guys asked. The general had gone below, and I was alone on the roof with two other soldiers. We held our breath. A faint whistling emerged from the fog.

"Incoming rocket!" I shouted and curled up. The whistling got louder. The rocket was heading straight toward us. We heard an enormous thud nearby followed by the sound of stone and shrapnel flying through the air.

"Fuck, that was close!" someone shouted. We stood to view the impact but couldn't spot anything through the thick fog. We could hear the general's voice below and could just barely see ghostly characters with weapons running to reinforce our positions along the front line. Then quiet. A couple minutes passed.

"Another one," one of the guys said calmly as we heard the familiar whistle yet again. This one also headed toward us. I couldn't believe their accuracy in the heavy fog. They must have aimed their rockets the day before. The rocket hit with a loud bang. ISIS was targeting the house and our post at the warehouse next door. An intense firefight broke out on our right flank. We couldn't see anything but heard gunfire in both directions. More rockets came our way. Some hit so close dirt and gravel rained down on us. The roof was flat with a brick parapet, so we were relatively well protected if we stayed low, but if a rocket hit the house, it would be game over for us.

I curled up in one corner and the others took the opposite side as rockets fired at two- or three-minute intervals, sometimes two at once. I had experienced intense shelling before, but nothing like this. At each new whistle, I shrank further into the corner and closed my eyes. It wasn't fun anymore.

Given their accuracy and intensity, I was convinced a rocket would hit us soon. So, this is how it ends. I thought of those back home. I hoped Susanne would cope with my death well, and that returning my body to Norway wouldn't be too costly for my family.

The warehouse was hit. I could hear shrapnel penetrating the metal roof after a rocket detonated inside. I was sure someone had been killed. I looked at my companions, despair on their faces. How long would this last? The general returned and shouted orders over the radio to the guys on the ground.

"Keep low and stay in your positions everyone!" He knelt next to me. His phone rang. I could hear President Barzani's voice on the other end. I knew it was serious if the president himself was calling.

"We are prepared, Mr. President. Nobody will get through the line," the general assured him. An hour and countless rockets later things finally calmed down. The firefight on our right flank had stopped. Eventually it got quiet on our side too.

The general was on the radio again insulting the Islamists. We knew ISIS listened in and our moods quickly recovered under his contagious fighting spirit. His challenge to the Islamists to attack us face to face made me grin. Incredibly, we had suffered no casualties, only damage to some of our vehicles and the warehouse. As the fog cleared, craters emerged around us. How had we survived?

Following the Sinjar operation, we were sent on many other missions. We searched Arab villages where inhabitants were suspected of collaborating with ISIS. Although we didn't find concrete evidence of their complicity, we seized many guns and distributed them among the unit.

We escorted the general to official meetings and events in Duhok and Erbil. I didn't care much for escort missions; they were boring, and I didn't enjoy the attention that came with accompanying the general.

A week after returning from Sinjar, the general was invited to make a speech at a boys' high school in Duhok. He was greeted like a rock star and awarded a trophy and medal in thanks for the victory in Sinjar. During his acceptance speech he suddenly called me to the stage. Confused, I joined him in full gear with my rifle hanging in front of my chest. His speech was in Badini, but I understood enough to get the point.

He told the boys I had come all the way from Norway to fight ISIS and that I had spent more time at the front than anyone else. After far more praise than I was comfortable with, he handed me the plastic trophy and medal, to the student's wild applause. My thoughts went back to the Akershus Fortress parade grounds a few months earlier. I had gotten my medal after all.

On our way out of the building we were barraged by cell-phone wielding students wanting to take pictures. I was used to that from escorting the general before, but this time they wanted pictures with me as well. After handfuls of boys took selfies with us, we finally made it outside where several hundred youth from other schools were blocking traffic in both directions. We had to fight our way through the adoring crowd.

"Wahed! Wahed! Wahed!" they chanted, as our unit formed a ring around the general and pushed our way to the vehicles. At one point I stumbled on the curb and was almost trampled by the jubilant crowd. We made it to our cars and with the help of the traffic police finally emerged onto the highway. I brushed dust from my uniform and promised myself I'd never work as a celebrity bodyguard. The general's phone rang.

"They did what? They killed who?" I looked quizzically at Deldar. The general was clearly upset and cursed loudly as he hung up the phone. He turned to us. "Deldar, call the rest of the Quick Reaction Force in Baqofah and tell them to bring all the squad weapons and meet us here. We're going back to Sinjar!"

Before we left Qabusiye, the general had promised its inhabitants he would sell them a truckload of sheep from Duhok. The sale would provide much-needed revenue for our unit and long-awaited meat for the villagers.

The truck with the sheep had left for Qabusiye that morning escorted by some of our men. They had been stopped in Sinjar by Yazidi militia and refused passage. The Yazidis accused the Qabusiye villagers of selling two hundred women and children to ISIS and were looking for revenge.

Maybe they saw an opportunity to get back at us as well. On our last day in Sinjar we had prevented Yazidi militia from plundering abandoned houses. It had ended in a physical confrontation and a Yazidi soldier had aimed his rifle at the general before being overpowered and arrested.

The Yazidis had been trained by - and worked with - the PKK. Many of the guys in my unit had fought against the PKK during the Kurdish civil war in the '90s and there was still much bad blood. Exactly what had transpired in Qabusiye was unclear, but we were told three of our guys had been shot and killed by the Yazidi militia and the escort team's weapons had been confiscated.

We waited for the rest of the Quick Reaction Force on the highway outside Duhok. The general was back on the phone, cursing loudly. Who had been killed? What would happen now? Several pickups loaded with troops and mounted machine guns pulled up. Soldiers jumped out of the vehicles and gathered around the general. Everyone looked grim and ready for battle.

After the general assessed our strength and firepower, we got back in our vehicles and headed for Sinjar. I took the passenger seat in one of the other SUVs.

"They killed Hassan! Those fuckers killed Hassan!" one of the guys in the backseat shouted. I turned around.

"Do you mean our Hassan?" Hassan lived in the room next to me. He was the most cheerful guy in the unit, and one of the most skillful. That summer we had built a dog house for the puppies together, and he had helped with feeding them. Was he really dead?

"Yes, our Hassan, they killed him. He is dead!" the infuriated soldier answered.

"We know you came here to fight Daesh, not other Kurds," he continued. "We can ask the general to drop you off before we reach Sinjar. Or do you want to support your brothers?"

Hassan had been not only a brother in arms, but a good friend. Was I willing to kill other Kurds over a conflict I didn't wish to be a part of? I thought long and hard as we sped toward Sinjar. I thought about Hassan. Pictures of him lying bloody and dying on the ground appeared in my head.

"I'm in," I finally said. An arm reached out and patted my shoulder.

"Good. We will show those fucking sons of bitches."

We could be dealing with as many as one hundred and fifty PKK-trained militia, and we were barely forty men. Should there be a firefight, it wouldn't end well.

We reached the first checkpoint before the Sinjar mountains. The general disappeared to make a phone call. The checkpoint was operated by the Peshmerga, but the soldiers were Yazidis and the atmosphere was tense. We were served tea; one of our guys whispered not to drink it. It could be poisoned.

"Enough," I thought. We were on the same side, after all. I took a sip and strolled over to the soldiers manning the checkpoint. They were burning trash to keep warm and I joined them. Although I wasn't religious, my family was Muslim and I had learned to respect others' beliefs, or lack thereof. The Yazidis weren't our enemy. I wished our guys would see that. But the militia who had killed our comrades had crossed the line, so retribution could be justified in my opinion.

The general was gone for a long time. It had gotten dark and the temperature had dropped noticeably. The fire had faded; the soldiers added the last pieces of garbage and a bottle of fuel. No one cared that the smoke was probably toxic, we just wanted to stay warm. One of our officers finally returned. We had to return to Baqofah. The president had heard about our mission, called the general, and ordered him to turn around. None of our guys had been killed.

"The Yazidis killed three shepherds from Qabusiye," The officer explained.

"So, Hassan is alive?"

"Yes, our people are safe," he said.

We drove back through Hatarah, the Yazidi village near our front. It was the middle of night and the streets were empty. As we passed, the backseat erupted in insults aimed at the PKK and the Yazidis. Before I went to Northern Iraq I knew little about internal conflicts among the Kurds. I knew that Peshmerga units under Masoud Barzani had battled the PKK and Peshmerga units led by Jalal Talabani during the Kurdish civil war in the '90s. The war had cost several thousand lives, both military and civilian. But that was almost twenty years ago, and I assumed the Kurds had united in the battle against ISIS and the region's oppressive regimes. But wounds of the civil war ran deep. Deldar had shown me a scar once.

"Do you see this? I got it when I was sixteen and the PKK marched into our village. They shot me in the leg because our village supported Barzani," he said. Another guy told me the PKK had killed his father during the civil war and that he hated the guerillas more than ISIS. Some Muslim Kurds had many prejudices against the Yazidis and their beliefs. I often heard Yazidis were dirty devil worshippers.

Yazidi militias had been accused of ethnic cleansing and revenge attacks against Arabs and Muslim Kurds in and around Sinjar. Many Muslim neighbors with whom Yazidis had lived for years exploited the situation, taking slaves and seizing Yazidi houses and other possessions. I could understand their anger, but ethnic cleansing couldn't be justified. A local expression says that Kurds are their own worst enemy. I couldn't have agreed more.

After the last week, I realized the battle for Sinjar was far from over.

13 WINTER

It was almost Christmas. I had planned to spend three or four months at the front, but when Susanne called and said her Christmas gift was a plane ticket home and she expected me there by Christmas Eve, I once again asked the general for a leave. I was granted a month off and, although I had only been at the front for a month, I looked forward to going home. I missed Susanne, and the conditions in Baqofah were as miserable as ever, with little food and sleepless nights.

The summer heat had been replaced with cold. Northern Iraqi winters can't be compared to Norway's, but we were constantly cold. Our only source of heat was one simple electric heater we shared inside the house. That the power was off for large chunks of the day didn't help matters. James and Tim visited one day.

"Do you need anything from Duhok?" Tim asked. They, like me, had started crowdfunding on social media, and had received substantial donations they would gladly spend on our unit.

"A couple of heaters would be nice," I answered while serving them tea. Tim promised to buy them.

A couple of days later I went on one last escort mission with the general before going home. We drove to a meeting at another front about an hour away. He entered a tent with several high-ranking officers and we stood guard outside. The atmosphere was relaxed as Saad showed me pictures on his phone. Suddenly, we heard an ominous whining.

On pure instinct we grabbed each other and dropped to the ground.

"What in the world was that?" I asked and looked over at Saad. It had sounded like an incoming mortar grenade passing just above our heads, but we heard no explosion. People began heading for the back of the tent.

A powerful 120mm grenade had landed next to it without detonating, just thirty yards from where Saad and I had stood. It had made a deep hole in the soft ground. A dozen soldiers stood around with flashlights taking pictures of the tailfin with their phones. The general came out, looked at the hole and scoffed before taking the rest of the officers back inside to continue the meeting. It was good we weren't the only ones equipped with low-quality ammunition.

On the road back to Baqofah we stopped at the top of the Bashiqa Mountain, which afforded an amazing view of the Nineveh plains below with Mosul in the distance. The general told us to wait by the vehicles as he walked to the edge of the mountain, lit a cigarette and looked thoughtfully across the plains. I wondered if he shared my dreams about Mosul.

A few days later I said farewell to the general, who stood outside the house feeding our dogs with chicken bought in one of the nearby villages. Kurds, like most Muslims, consider dogs unclean and usually keep them at bay by throwing rocks at them or kicking them if they get too close. But not when the general, also a dog lover, or I were present.

"You feed the dogs better than us," our cook Adel complained.

"That's because I like the dogs better than you," the general answered with a grin.

One of the guys drove me to Duhok where we met James and Tim, who had bought six heaters for us. My driver grinned from ear to ear.

"This should keep your nuts warm at night," James said. I translated for the driver but left out the nuts. We thanked the Brits and drove on to the cab station. Because there is no public transportation in the country, cabs are the only form of transport other than private vehicles.

Two hours later I arrived in Erbil and checked into a hotel. Just as the Norwegian military arranged a stopover for returning soldiers, I had my own stopover to ensure my transition to life back in Norway would go smoothly. Karl Håkon had traveled from Kirkuk to see me and had checked into the same hotel. We met in the lobby that evening for tea and a chat. I was curious about his last couple of months. Not surprisingly, he had been mostly at a base in Kirkuk with a small group of Western volunteers training with local forces.

"Our instructor is an Italian named Alex," Karl Håkon said. "He is very skilled, but you get tired of just training all the time."

I knew of Alex. He had contacted me earlier to involve Agit and me in a business endeavor. Agit had shown interest, and with the president's nephew on board there was a good chance of realizing Alex's plan to build Northern Iraq's largest and most advanced tactical training center. I had bowed out since my unit had been my first priority.

The next day, Karl Håkon and I went to the market, my favorite place in Erbil. Small shops, stalls, restaurants and teahouses were crammed together forming a labyrinth. We were surrounded by fresh fruits and vegetables, meat and fish, nuts, spices, honey and cheese, traditional Kurdish clothes, jewelry and ornaments. It was like traveling back in time, less the cheap Chinese electronics. I could have easily spent an entire day at the market, looking at the goods, studying the people and tasting different sweets and freshly pressed juices.

Nearby, an ancient fortress sat atop an enormous mound. It was popular among the few tourists who found their way to Erbil, so I took Karl Håkon with me for a look. According to archaeologists and historians, the site had been inhabited continuously for nearly eight thousand years; a fascinating thought.

We walked up the long, steep hill to the empty fortress and were winded when we reached the top. Begrudgingly I had to admit I was out of shape after nearly a year on a poor diet with no cardiovascular training. As I watched the ground to avoid one of many puddles, I heard Norwegian being spoken. I looked up to see Dilshad and two other Norwegians approaching. Dilshad was dressed as a civilian; the two others were nicely dressed and carrying laptop bags and document folders. I could tell they were military intelligence, and Dilshad was apparently their interpreter. He had served as an interpreter in the Telemark Battalion's first contingent, but it wasn't unusual for soldiers and officers with special skills to be offered back-to-back deployments, likely the case here. To avoid trouble for him, I only greeted him briefly as we passed. The world is a really small place sometimes.

I was back in Norway by December 16. It was wonderful seeing Susanne again. As we had the year before, we spent Christmas Eve at my place, just the two of us. We didn't need anyone else. We lived in our own happy bubble, making holiday cakes and watching Christmas movies. In the new year I visited family and friends, including Eivind, who had left the Telemark Battalion and would head for Sulaymaniyah in February to volunteer at one of the city's hospitals. I wondered if anyone at Rena was suspicious. He didn't think so.

We agreed to meet in Sulaymaniyah in the spring. I was in regular contact with Knut, whom Eivind and I had met in Oslo some months earlier. He was still set on joining the YPG in Syria, but his friend had gotten cold feet and had withdrawn from the plan.

"The YPG told me to wait, since the border crossings they use are closed right now," He said. "But I'm ready, and I'll leave as soon as they tell me to."

During my leave I bought large quantities of medical supplies paid for by Instagram followers. I chose material I knew the unit could use with only basic training and packed it in sets in individual plastic bags; tourniquet, bandages, rubber gloves, and wound cleaning supplies, simple stuff that could save a life if used correctly. Donations kept coming in and I also bought much needed night optics.

I celebrated my birthday in Oslo with Susanne in the middle of January. We ate out and checked into a hotel to spend our last night together before I had to leave for the front again. My impending departure subdued the occasion. Like the previous time, Susanne was in full tears as we said goodbye. I felt like the world's worst boyfriend, leaving her alone, not knowing if she would ever see me alive again.

Back in Baqofah, I learned ISIS had launched a massive offensive on several fronts, including ours, on the day I left for Norway. Coalition aircraft had bombed advancing Islamists before they reached the front line, and our guys had retrieved weapons and ammunition from dead ISIS fighters in no man's land. Not everyone had been as lucky. At a nearby front, the enemy had broken through and killed several Peshmerga soldiers.

Saad showed me a propaganda video ISIS had posted online after the attack: Islamists calmly walked around a demolished settlement where Peshmerga forces had stayed before the attack, tearing down Kurdish flags. It could just as easily have been Baqofah. I was reminded that constant vigilance was critical, even inside our village.

While I was on leave, French special forces had spent several days at our front, using our house as a base of operations to call in airstrikes against ISIS in the south. In a matter of days, French jets had dropped more than one hundred bombs over the neighboring towns of Batnaya and Tel Keppe. Then the French had packed their bags and gone to another front to do the same again. It was clear the French were out for revenge for the terror attack in Paris.

James and Tim were gone. Tim had rejoined his group in Kirkuk and James had followed. Not long after, their group disbanded and both James and Tim returned home.

We learned that one of their leaders, a Brit named Barry Hall, was wanted for rape in his homeland.

The heaters James and Tim had bought us had been divided between our two houses in Baqofah. Since electricity was mostly out during the day, we kept a fire going in an empty oil barrel we'd poked holes in with a pick. We placed the home-made oven next to the guard post outside the general's house and stood around it drinking tea and talking until late in the evening when power returned.

We raided the village daily for fuel. With an axe we chopped up anything that would burn; furniture, doors, cabinets and window shutters. We burned anything made of wood or paper and when we ran out we went to the neighboring village.

One day Nahman and I picked up two young soldiers from the front line to help gather wood in an abandoned village. Nahman, one of the most experienced and skilled guys in our unit, had been there before and knew exactly where to look. The guys called him Ali Baba for his constant plundering. We split into two teams and went in separate directions. Nahman and I went together.

The next village, a little more than one thousand yards away, was controlled by ISIS and it didn't take long before a rocket detonated with a deafening bang inside the village we were raiding. The two young guys came running back, covered in dust and sand.

"What happened?" Nahman asked.

"The rocket hit right next to us! Those motherfuckers!" They seemed physically unharmed but were in shock. We continued our work under sporadic fire; we had experienced worse things.

It had been almost a year since I joined Wahed Kovle's unit. During that time the number of soldiers under his command had more than halved. At the end of January, one of his most experienced officers took sixteen soldiers and joined another unit that was better off than ours. It was a hard blow to us and to the general. He had sacrificed so much in the war against ISIS and had gotten little in return. While I had been in Norway the general had sold some of our weapons, including the MG1 machine gun I used, to raise funds for the unit.

I volunteered to take shifts at the front line again, which was now dangerously undermanned. From six in the evening to six in the morning, several times a week, I sat on guard in one of the recently unmanned positions. As usual we were engaged by indirect fire a couple of times each day, and sometimes we answered with our own mortars or heavy machine guns. Now and then we sighted ISIS fighters on reconnaissance missions or trying to infiltrate our front.

One night we spotted four Islamists on a small knoll in no man's land just 600- to 700-yards from us. We could thank our donated night optics for the observation. The enemy disappeared behind the rise before we could hit them, but it didn't take long for a Coalition jet to show up and start circling above us. The goat lovers behind the knoll must have realized they had been seen and were about meet their maker. I opened a can of Wild Tiger and waited for the jet to attack. After circling a few times, the jet approached at a low altitude. The explosion's flash reached us first. Two seconds later, the sound and shockwave penetrated my body. The pilots get all the fun, I thought, as I downed my energy drink.

On the one-year anniversary of my arrival in Baqofah, the village took heavy shelling. In less than two hours, we were hit with more than twenty-five 120mm grenades and had to seek refuge in the neighboring house. Ayhan, who was barely twenty and new to the Quick Reaction Force, thought he saw a grenade land in a field behind the village without detonating.

A couple of hours after the attack, lacking anything better to do, he and I went to look for the grenade. I looked over at Batnaya, hoping ISIS wouldn't see us out in the open. We quickly realized this had been a bad idea, and Ayhan suggested we return to the village. We had retreated only a few steps when we heard an incoming grenade. Reflexively, I threw myself to the ground and covered my head. The grenade hit close by and small lumps of dirt pelted me. I looked over to Ayhan, who had also fallen to the ground.

"Ayhan, are you okay? Ayhan? Ayhan!" I ran to his motionless body, convinced he had been hit in the head by shrapnel. I grabbed him. He stared at me vacantly and mumbled incomprehensibly. He was in shock, but alive and otherwise unharmed.

"Come, we must go back before they fire more grenades," I said as I helped him to his feet. We stumbled across the field and it hit us. We were alive! We were alive, and it felt great. We broke into spontaneous laughter as we ran, like two little boys caught stealing apples.

Later that evening we went back to find Ayhan's sunglasses, which he'd dropped when he hit the ground. We found them and measured the distance to the crater. Fifty yards. This was the second time in a few months I had survived a 120mm grenade that landed within a radius that usually caused death or major injury. This time I had survived only because the soft dirt absorbed the grenade's force and most of the shrapnel. On a harder surface, it would not have ended well.

Despite increasing action at the front, I still hadn't experienced direct combat and it bothered me. A year had passed. I asked myself how much longer I could keep taking indirect fire without being able to retaliate. Little did I know my first exam as a fighting soldier was just two days away.

14 BATTLE-TESTED

I was texting Susanne one evening when some of the guys ran into the house and grabbed their weapons and ammunition.

"What's going on?" I asked.

"We don't know," one replied. "The general asked us to bring weapons and meet him at the checkpoint outside Hatarah. We have enough guys, so you can stay here since you have the day off."

It wasn't unusual for the Quick Reaction Force to be called without explanation. Most likely it was just another escort mission. A calm evening on the phone with Susanne was tempting. Still, I didn't want to risk missing something important.

"I'm in, just let me get dressed. Don't leave without me!" I shouted. I texted Susanne that I would be gone for the rest of the evening, without explaining why, logged off the Fastlink and jumped into the waiting vehicle, knowing I'd face her wrath the following day.

We drove full speed toward the checkpoint. The general smiled when he saw me and ordered me into his SUV. This might be more than just another escort mission, I thought. We headed west with the general driving, as always. Deldar rode shotgun and Nahman and I sat in the back. While the general was on the phone I leaned over to Nahman and asked if he knew where we were going. He grinned and mimed shooting using his hands. I leaned back and looked out the window. I wasn't going to get my hopes up. I had been on too many false alarms before.

We arrived at the Mosul Dam, which ISIS had conquered during their August 2014 offensive. The Islamists had controlled the critical dam for almost two weeks before Peshmerga forces reclaimed it. As we crossed the dam, the general recounted that battle, in which he and his brother Akram had fought.

"Here I drove off the road, crashed and shot a guy from Daesh at close range when he tried to get into the car," the general eagerly told us. Whenever he talked about his dead brother, he cried. Deldar found a handkerchief. The general was proof sensitivity and toughness can coexist.

We reached the village of Aski Mosul, south of the dam, where we learned our assignment. Intelligence claimed ISIS was planning a massive attack against the Aski Mosul front during the night and the general didn't want to miss out on a good fight. After a brief meeting with the unit we would support, we left the village and drove to the nearby front line.

From the front line, a road led to an outpost in no man's land the size of a football pitch with sandbag and dirt walls and concrete guard towers on each corner. A trench filled with barbed wire enclosed the perimeter, but it was far narrower and shallower than the trench at our front. The enemy could easily cross with vehicles and on foot.

We prepared to repel the incoming attack. I was assigned to one of the guard towers with two of the local guys. They told me their unit was comprised of Syrian Kurds who had escaped from the civil war in the neighboring country. They had established their own unit in Northern Iraq, consisting of several thousand men under the command of President Masoud Barzani. Their dialect was easier to understand than Badini, the one my guys spoke, and we quickly hit it off.

Hours went by with no signs of activity from the two nearest villages, both controlled by ISIS. Was the intelligence wrong? As twilight fell, a massive explosion on our left flank heralded tracers flying in all directions.

"Here we go," I thought.

ISIS attacked our neighboring unit, less than one and a half mile from us. We responded with intense shooting from our heavy machine guns and lighter squad weapons. I left the guard tower and positioned myself at the opposite side of the outpost for a better view. White trails erupted from one of the neighboring villages. ISIS had fired rockets and they were headed for us.

"Stay low, people!" the general shouted. Rockets flew above us and hit the village we had inhabited earlier with deafening bangs. I pointed my scope at the attacking village. More rockets landed around us. So far, the outpost had avoided any direct hits. Mortar fire from the second village was followed by cannon attacks from both. Two of the local boys readied our only mortar, a small 60mm weapon. I knelt next to them. The battle raged at such a distance I couldn't do anything with my rifle, so I turned on my helmet camera and documented the action. We dropped our first 60mm grenade into the tube, aiming at the neighboring village.

"Too short!" The general shouted. The soldiers adjusted the tube.

"Better, but more towards the left this time!" the general corrected.

After the third grenade both soldiers bolted toward the nearest guard tower. Before I could react, a grenade struck an empty water tank right outside the outpost, less than fifteen yards away. Wreckage and dirt showered me. If the grenade had landed one yard to the side, all three of us would have been peppered with shrapnel. Once again, I had escaped death by the slightest margin.

I burst into laughter. You never feel as alive as you do after a near-death experience; you've been given a second chance in life. With the relief and the adrenaline rush, I was having the time of my life. It is scary how addictive war can be.

The shelling continued for hours. I moved from position to position hoping to find enemy fighters within shooting distance, but the fire seemed to come only from the two distant villages. I spotted a stray dog sitting on top of the berm facing no man's land, completely exposed to incoming fire. I shouted, and the dog ran to me, wagging its tale. In the middle of battle, I cuddled with a dog, and smiled.

My attention was quickly diverted to one of the locals on a pickup shooting a mounted 14.5mm machine gun towards the neighboring village.

"What are you shooting?" I asked. He indicated a point in the village.

"There's a 23mm machine cannon there, shooting at us," he said. "Can you see it?" I couldn't spot it with my naked eye, but I could hear its projectiles hurtling above us. I aimed my scope at the fire's origin and picked up the machine cannon's muzzle. It was far. I doubted there was any point in firing at it, even with our heavy machine gun.

We heard a sharp explosion in the air just a few yards away and jumped for cover. 23mm shells are explosive, made to detonate either on impact or after being in the air for a set time. This one had come in much lower than the previous ones. Had it not exploded midair, it could have hit us. How much luck did I have left?

A PKM machine gun opened fire from the opposite side of the outpost with a long, continuous volley. I ran over and found the general manning the gun.

"There are Daesh in the grass!" he shouted. My pulse spiked. I lay down behind the sandbags and searched for ISIS with my scope, my hunting instinct turned on. Several guys opened fire. It was impossible to see what they were shooting.

"Where are they?" I shouted. No one gave me a good answer. A lone projectile hit a sandbag in front of me, sending dirt flying. I threw myself down.

"Don't stick your head up. They are zeroed in," I said to the guy next to me as I moved to another position.

Again, a solitary bullet hit right in front of me. Single shots worried me. Amateurs usually shoot volleys in all directions. This shooter seemed well trained, staying low in the terrain and delivering precise individual shots. I was convinced the shooter was moving from position to position. I did the same but was constantly forced down by the enemy. They were difficult to locate and skilled, I would grant them that.

Deldar had taken my spot in the guard tower and the general stood below, readying an anti-tank weapon. An armored truck had been observed in one of the neighboring villages, and we feared it was a suicide vehicle headed our way. Shots rang out on all sides as grenades and rockets rained down over the outpost. As the unit's media representative, Saad filmed it all with his phone. Suddenly he stumbled and dropped his phone, clutching his neck. Adel and Bakhtiar ran over and grabbed him.

They ran with him toward the field kitchen and I followed. We stopped outside and I tried to evaluate his injury. Saad lifted his hand from his neck; blood shot out and hit Bakhtiar in the face. I applied pressure to the wound, a small shrapnel hole, and felt warm, sticky blood trickle down my hands. Bakhtiar took a bandage from the kit I'd given him.

"Get the bandage on now!" I said while calming Saad. He was in shock and struggled to stand, shouting that we had to help the general. Bakhtiar lost his temper.

"Shut the fuck up and never mind Wahed!" he shouted. "Sit still so we can help you!"

An officer from the unit we were supporting watched and seemed worried. I asked if they had called for an ambulance. He assured me it was on its way.

After bandaging the wound, Bakhtiar and I remained with Saad. He was pale as a ghost from all the blood he had lost. I knew well how terrible Kurdish field hospitals were. Their medical staff's skill was equally lacking. When the ambulance drove off with Saad I didn't know if I would see him alive again. We later learned that an ISIS sniper in the grass had glimpsed Saad through a small opening in the sandbags. He had missed his target, but the projectile hit the concrete guard tower and shrapnel hit Saad.

Intense fire rang on all sides. I remained outside the field kitchen and looked at my blood-soaked hands. Reality dawned; I might not leave the outpost alive.

"I am of no use sitting here," I thought. I wiped my palms on my uniform, picked up my rifle and ran back to the battlement.

The suspected suicide vehicle we had observed earlier in the neighboring village was a bulldozer, and it was heading for us. Its slow speed indicated it might be reinforced with heavy steel plates and carrying a lot of explosives, a widespread ISIS tactic. At least it would take a while to reach us.

I focused on finding enemy in the grass. During my last stay in Norway, an American follower had sent me a new rifle scope, significantly better than my old one. When one of the local guys pointed to advancing ISIS fighters, it didn't take long to get them in my sights. In a ditch about 350 yards from the outpost, three enemy fighters moved up and down as they took shots at us. I took a deep breath. It was finally happening. I was about to directly engage the enemy.

I went into autopilot. I had done the drill thousands of times. I rested my rifle on a sandbag with my left hand in between for extra recoil control and grip. I wrapped my right hand firmly around the pistol grip, settled the stock against my shoulder and pushed my upper body forward. Lastly, I leaned my cheek on the stock and peered through the scope as I tried to control my breathing. I flipped the safety off and calculated the distance. It was perhaps a bit too far, considering the targets were constantly moving, but it was worth a try. I eased my finger onto the trigger and squeezed.

The bullet left the barrel at supersonic speed, hitting right in front of the ditch. I adjusted my scope and took another shot. I had filled my magazines so the first round, and every fifth round, was a tracer to track my projectiles' paths.

It was hard to gauge the bullet's impact through the grass, but the next tracer confirmed I was on target. I hit right in the ditch and kept shooting, one shot at a time, calm and controlled. Had I hit anyone? The targets disappeared, then reappeared close by. Or were there more than just three enemy in the ditch? Either way, they would be extremely uncomfortable. Pinning the enemy down is an important tactic. Bullets flew in both directions and incoming fire hit the sandbags in front of us. The guy next to me was none too eager to poke his head up and return fire.

"Here, use my PKM," he offered. I had already used several of my own magazines and knew the battle could last all day, so I gladly took his machine gun and emptied the belt into the enemy ditch. The ditch was still. Either the targets were dead, or they had retreated.

I looked for new targets and spotted an ISIS fighter lying in the grass about 250 yards away. He was easily visible to everyone and the shooting began. I opened fire. Dirt flew as our bullets hit around him. He jerked, rolled around a couple of times then lay lifeless on the ground. I knelt to change my magazine. We had another problem.

"The bulldozer is coming, get ready!" the general shouted hoarsely. We now faced the most terrifying weapon in the ISIS arsenal. The bulldozer would probably try to scour a path into our outpost before blowing itself up. Our chances of surviving would be zero. The general, sensing his men's faltering spirits, gathered us for a pep talk.

"When that bulldozer comes, you will stay here and fight like men!" He roared. "No matter what happens, we stay and fight. Do you understand? We are Peshmerga, those who face death. We know no fear! Long live Peshmerga!" Fear and insecurity evaporated. No one could motivate their soldiers like the general. I would follow this man to Hell and back.

"Long live Peshmerga!" we shouted at full force. The general walked back to the wall, picked up a rocket-propelled grenade launcher and aimed at the bulldozer.

Our machine guns were trained on the intruder too, but bullets would simply bounce off the steel plates. The general's first rocket hit its target.

The armored beast lumbered on. The general fired more rockets. Despite repeated hits, the bulldozer continued unfazed.

Death rumbled slowly toward us. There was nothing we could do. We were fucked. Less than fifty yards from the outpost, the bulldozer got stuck in the trench. The driver tried desperately to back up. Another rocket hit the vehicle. I knelt behind the wall. There was nothing to do but pray. The driver must have realized he was defeated. No more than a stone's throw from the outpost he blew up the vehicle and himself. The massive explosion filled the air with sand and dust. Guys were thrown backwards and the windows on the nearest cars shattered from the shockwave. The guy next to me was knocked over. I grabbed his arm.

"Are you okay, Buddy?" I asked. He nodded. I used hearing protection during firefights, a habit I'd developed in the Norwegian armed forces, so the explosion didn't affect me as much as the others, who crawled around on the ground, disoriented. The sand and dust settled, and they got to their feet. We were alive. The bulldozer was destroyed. A large crater was all that remained. We raised our rifles in the air and shouted, "Long live Peshmerga!"

But the battle wasn't over. ISIS kept up the attack with rockets, mortar grenades, machine cannons and sniper fire from the grass. From the wall I tried locating more enemy fighters in front of us. The air was filled with bullets.

"Man down!" Deldar yelled from the guard tower. A couple of us ran to catch a man being lowered from the tower. We dragged him to a pickup truck. The soldier, with whom I had spent the night in the guard tower, had been shot through the head by a sniper. One of his friends applied pressure to the wound with his hand. It was obvious the man was dead. The truck drove off with the lifeless body, his friend enfolding him.

I didn't have time to contemplate that a human being I had gotten to know just the night before had been killed. The battle was raging, and another armored vehicle was headed for us. I got into one of the positions for a better view of the situation. An armored military personnel carrier sped toward us with a manned machine gun on the roof. I felt helpless with my M16 rifle. What could I do? The general hit the vehicle with a rocket, but it forged on. I was hit by a panic I had never experienced before. I fled my position and took cover behind a vehicle. I was convinced the suicide vehicle would obliterate the outpost. At the wall, the general readied another anti-tank rocket. He was fearless.

"What the fuck are you doing, Mike?" I thought. "Get your shit together!" I took a deep breath and ran back to the position.

The general's rocket finally stopped the vehicle one hundred yards away. The side door of the burning personnel carrier opened and four ISIS fighters were gunned down as they emerged. The vehicle was engulfed in flames. Black smoke belched out the side door and roof hatch. Could anyone still be alive in there? A fighter jet finally arrived and circled above us.

"A little late, buddy," I thought.

Suddenly, an ISIS fighter jumped out of the vehicle and raced back towards the village. I switched off my safety, aimed my scope ahead of the enemy and fired. One shot, two shots, three shots. Others opened fire. He dropped. At this distance I could see his facial features, unlike the enemy earlier in the day. It felt no different. In fact, I felt nothing at all. I had thought I would feel something the first time I shot at another human with the intent to kill, but I was numb. Would emotion arrive later?

Another ISIS fighter ran from the vehicle. This guy had thrown away his weapon and his combat vest to run faster. It didn't matter. He too went down, but he didn't fall fast. The sequence reminded me of a marathon runner crossing the finish line and gradually dropping to his knees in exhaustion.

I changed out my magazine and looked around. Reinforcements had arrived from other units. I recognized some of the black, armored vehicles slowly rolling into the outpost as the Kurdish special forces I had met during the Sinjar offensive. It was good to see them again. We had regained the upper hand. The jet that had been circling above us for a couple of minutes fired a missile without warning and struck a couple of hundred yards from the outpost. A sniper's body flew high in the air, spinning like a rag doll. Our spirits were improving.

One of our bulldozers cleared a path into no man's land and several armored vehicles, including the general's, followed to find any Islamists remaining in the grass. The rest of us stayed at the outpost; I found a good position to watch. The first vehicle had driven barely one hundred yards before it stopped. The top cover pointed his AK-47 rifle at a point just a few yards away and emptied an entire magazine into a hiding sniper. He grabbed the .50 caliber machine gun on the roof, pointed it at the same spot and fired several bursts so powerful that dirt and chunks of flesh flew into the air. It was a satisfactory ending.

The shooting gradually died out. Two more ISIS fighters were killed near the outpost, probably the same guys who had taken shots at me earlier. I followed a couple soldiers into no man's land to inspect the area. The armored personnel carrier was completely engulfed in flames. Bodies lay scattered around. Nearly twenty ISIS fighters had been killed around our outpost. We later learned that about four hundred ISIS soldiers had fought in the failed offensive against the Aski Mosul front. Almost one quarter had been killed.

In the trench two dead Islamists lay next to each other, caught in the barbed wire. Local troops were already looting the corpses. I grabbed my phone to take a picture. One of the soldiers spotted me, grabbed one of the terrorists by his hair and lifted his head, posing proudly. I took a photo, thanked the soldier and returned to the outpost. The previous year, media in Norway had run a story on the Norwegian forces' concern about exactly those type of pictures being taken by the Peshmerga they were training. I thought pictures were a better souvenir than body parts, which wasn't uncommon in war.

Eventually our job was complete. We said farewell to the unit we had supported and set our course for Baqofah. It was a blustery ride. Our windshield had been blown away by the explosion and cold wind rushed through the car as our speed increased. I covered my face with a scarf and reflected on the day's events. I had finally experienced real combat, the good and the bad. I had seen people die, felt fear and victory. I had been fired at and returned fire. I had survived. I was finally battle-tested.

15 HIRANI

A few days after the battle at Aski Mosul, I returned to Norway on my third leave. But first I visited my aunt in Sulaymaniyah, my birthplace. I had been a young boy when she last visited my family in Norway. I was excited and looked forward to seeing the city my family had left thirty years earlier.

In Sulaymaniyah I met Karl Håkon, whom I had invited to stay at my aunt's place until I left for Norway. We each got a mattress on the living room floor and the clean, calm surroundings were a respite after two months at the front. After a good night's sleep, we went to the local hospital where Eivind had been working as a volunteer nurse for about a month. Since we'd last spoken, Karl Håkon had found a new unit at a front just south of Kirkuk. It was relatively quiet there, and he still seemed bored.

Eivind, on the other hand, had his hands full. All hospitals in Sulaymaniyah had closed during the Kurdish Region's economic crisis, except for this one. Eivind was very skilled and knowledgeable compared to the locals. He had earned a lot of trust and was working with many patients. He spoke of bad injuries and patients who died during treatment, but he seemed content. He was finally getting the experience he craved.

The three of us toured the city. Sulaymaniyah reminded me of Duhok, encircled by mountains, buzzing with life. We ate kebab, drank tea and played pool. I tried to imagine my life if my parents hadn't fled Northern Iraq. Would I have job during this time of crisis? What about a family? Would I even be alive? I was grateful we had escaped.

Knut met us at my aunt's place, where he would also stay for a couple of days. He had joined the YPG and was waiting for transport to Syria. After Knut unpacked and got his own mattress on the living room floor, we took a cab to one of the shopping malls.

The place was enormous and exquisitely decorated, with prices equal to those in Norway, if not higher. The wealthier population shopped here for brand name clothes and the latest smartphones, drinking coffee macchiato and freshly pressed juice. As we strolled around in climate-controlled comfort, it was hard to believe a war raged just a few miles away.

We found a place to eat and each ordered a hamburger. Knut seemed subdued by the gravity of his situation, the reality of finally being here. He struggled to finish his meal. A few days later he abandoned his plan to go to Syria and joined Karl Håkon's unit.

After a week in Sulaymaniyah I left the guys, parked my guns and equipment with my aunt, and headed for the airport.

I spent most of my time at home with Susanne. It felt like the best time of my life up to that point. We baked, cooked and went for long walks, followed by coffee, hot chocolate and pastries from the local gas station. My time at the front had taught me to appreciate the small things in life - things most people take for granted.

At the same time, I prepared for my trip back to Iraq. I filled my bags with medical supplies and other essentials for the guys in the unit. For Saad, who had survived his injury from Aski Mosul, I bought a helmet camera, so he wouldn't have to risk his life filming with his phone.

I uploaded a video of the battle from my helmet camera. It caught the attention of foreign media and went viral. Before I knew it, I had tens of thousands of new Instagram followers. The American company that produced my rifle scope saw the video. That I used their scope in combat was a big deal for a company who sold products intended for sport shooting. They offered to send a few thousand dollars' worth of scopes and other products. The endorsement I had given their products was likely worth a lot more.

Back in Sulaymaniyah I picked up my equipment and thanked my aunt for her hospitality. Like the rest of my family, she wasn't happy with my plans to participate in the Mosul offensive. She tried convincing me to return to Norway for good, but I was dead set on taking part in Mosul's liberation and seeing the end of ISIS' reign of terror in Iraq. I assured her I would be fine and that we most likely wouldn't enter the city itself, although I hoped for just the opposite.

I had other business in Sulaymaniyah as well. A few months earlier, a Kurdish Swede named Hirani had contacted me through Instagram. Like many others, he had asked to join my unit. Although I avoided recommending Westerners to the general, I had made an exception for Hirani because of his Kurdish roots. When Hirani was ten, his heartbroken mother had sent him and his older brother to live with his father in Sweden, but not until Hirani had witnessed horrendous war crimes against his people. Hirani had already served nearly a year in another Peshmerga unit in Kirkuk. Company from Scandinavia was tempting.

My cab stopped outside the house where Hirani and his mother waited. I promised his mother I would take good care of her boy. Hirani was young and I immediately felt responsible for him. I hoped I could send him back to Sweden alive and unharmed once our job was done. We got into the cab and headed for Kirkuk, the first stop on our way to Baqofah.

Along the way I noticed Hirani kept looking over at me, smiling nervously.

"What is it?" I asked.

"Well, you aren't quite like I imagined," He replied. I had to smile. I had heard this before.

"Let me guess. You imagined a six foot five, broad-shouldered, loud-mouthed war-junkie thirsting for blood and war?" We both laughed. Social media easily gave that impression, but I am quite the opposite; calm and understated by nature, not the most talkative or the loudest.

I asked Hirani about his previous unit. He said he had left Sweden at eighteen to join the Peshmerga when ISIS occupied the Kurdish areas in Northern Iraq in 2014. As he was a young foreigner, he had been overprotected.

"I had to sneak out on most operations," he said. "I hid in the back of the pickup truck. Once we were there they couldn't send me back." Hirani had seen things few Swedish teenagers had. "Once we drove into a Peshmerga-controlled village that Daesh had attacked," he said. "There were bodies everywhere.

"We passed a car in flames with two Peshmerga soldiers burnt black as coal. Their lips were burned off, completely exposing their white teeth. I will never forget that. When we returned to base the guys had yogurt like nothing had happened, while I threw up." Hirani was clearly upset by recalling the incident. I started thinking perhaps he was too young for this game and wondered if I had made a mistake by recruiting him.

In Kirkuk we were greeted by Swedish Jesper, who had become a celebrity in Sweden after spending time in Syria with the YPG. After leaving Syria, he had joined a Peshmerga unit west of Kirkuk and was allowed to recruit other Western volunteers. I had put him in touch with Karl Håkon, and Karl Håkon, Knut and Eivind had joined this new group, known as the Scandinavian Group. I had agreed to help them recruit more Scandinavians through social media, but first I wanted to see their working conditions. Jesper made a good impression as we drove to their front. He talked a lot but seemed like a guy who got shit done. Karl Håkon, Knut and Eivind greeted us at their front.

"How was Norway?" Eivind asked. It was weird seeing him in uniform again.

"Can't complain," I answered.

Hirani and I would spend three days here before traveling on, so we each got a bed in a shack the Scandinavians had for themselves. Jesper showed me around. I was impressed by what I saw. As one of few Western groups allowed at the front line, they had their own guard post with squad weapons and seemed to have established good routines after only a couple of weeks. Eivind had his own ambulance and infirmary plus responsibility for the unit's battlefield medicine.

"There's not too much going on here, but we get many refugees who have escaped from ISIS controlled areas," Eivind explained. "They often carry their dead and wounded who stepped on land mines or were shot by ISIS. They don't spare anyone, not even the children." I couldn't fathom how anyone could shoot fleeing civilians, especially children. While we talked, several local soldiers asked Eivind to examine various wounds and ailments. Although there was little fighting on this front, Eivind, who had been nicknamed "Doctor" by the locals, had plenty to do.

Knut, who had been a construction worker in Norway, spent his time improving the Scandinavian part of the front line. Jesper was constantly occupied arranging visits from local and international press, to the great frustration of his compatriots. Overall, I was impressed, and I promised Jesper to promote the group. I also recommended they be very selective about who they accepted into the unit. Many other Western groups had been disbanded because of a few rotten apples. It would be a shame if that happened here.

"You should have relevant military experience as a minimum requirement," I suggested before Hirani and I left.

Back in Baqofah I introduced Hirani to the unit and fixed him a bed in my room. He was well received by the general, as I had been the previous year.

"As you know, Mike, we don't usually accept foreigners in this unit. But if you can vouch for him, that's good enough for me," he had said. More than ever I hoped Hirani could cope with life at the front. It would damage the trust I had built with general over the past year if Hirani didn't function as a part of the unit.

I brought him with me on guard duty at the front line and taught him our routines. I got time to know him better. When he immigrated to Sweden with his brother they had lived in a troubled area of Stockholm. He had gotten involved with gangs at a young age and had many regrets. The war had saved him. During his time with the Peshmerga Hirani had severed all contact with the bad influences back home. He seemed like a genuinely good kid who had been dealt an unlucky hand.

That he lacked military experience was obvious. On one of our first night shifts at the front line he started playing loud music on his phone, nodding his head to the rap beat without a care in the world. I looked at him in disbelief.

"Hirani, are you even going to hear anything if someone starts shooting at us?" I asked. He turned off the music but seemed slightly annoyed. The front had been quiet the entire night, but just a few minutes later we heard an incoming mortar grenade and ducked for cover. The grenade struck less than twenty yards from us, and the shrapnel shot just over our heads. We looked at each other and laughed.

"Would you have heard that coming with your music on?" I demanded. Hirani never played music again. He was willing to learn and took counsel. It didn't take long before I trusted him more than I did the local guys, who could be sloppy when handling weapons and explosives.

"The day we advance to Mosul, I will be more afraid of being shot by our own than by the enemy," I told Hirani confidentially.

"I know what you mean," he replied. "I felt like that in Kirkuk, with unsecured weapons and fingers on triggers on every operation. I've lost count of how many unintentional discharges I witnessed." In the Norwegian armed forces, unintentional discharges are taken extremely seriously, and usually lead to punishment and a fine. The Kurds, on the other hand, shrug it off if no one was hurt. While I had been on leave at home, several of our unit's soldiers had been wounded by indirect fire.

We started seeing increased enemy activity. ISIS appeared to be mapping out our front using both commercial drones, which were cheap and easy to use, and reconnaissance teams that snuck around no man's land at night. One night through our night optics we spotted two teams of fourteen enemy fighters creeping toward our front. A coalition jet appeared and annihilated the Islamists in front of us. The increased enemy activity made some of the guys think something big was brewing. Was ISIS planning a major attack?

The alarm sounded on the night of May 3. As I dressed, I assured Hirani this was normal. We hopped into a pickup, rode to the front line at full speed and got into position.

"What's going on?" I asked one of the guys as I popped a can of Wild Tiger.

"Someone saw Daesh in no man's land, but I don't know," he said. "It's been quiet all night." I turned to Hirani.

"If you want to last long at this front you need to be patient," I said. "We probably won't see action before the Mosul offensive in the fall." I couldn't have been more wrong.

It was the day all Hell broke loose. It was the day ISIS burned oil to hinder Coalition planes. It was the day the general was on vacation in

Beirut. It was the day ISIS laid a bridge across our trench. And, it was the day I ran toward our fleeing neighboring unit's position, straight to the enemy.

16 THE FRONT IS BROKEN

What was I really thinking, as I ran all alone towards the point from which hundreds of heavily armed soldiers had just fled? In my mind the Peshmerga were fearless warriors who would rather die than turn tail. The neighboring unit's actions were shameful. Perhaps I thought my initiative would inspire them to come back. At the very least I hoped my own guys would follow me. I had run two hundred yards, halfway there, when I turned and saw my team where I had left them, beckoning me back. It was out of the question.

Over the last two months I had been haunted by the memory of the brief moment in Aski Mosul when I had panicked and hidden behind a vehicle. It had taken only a minute to regain my composure and run back to my position, but I was ashamed.

"If the general were here now he would do the same," I thought as I ran alone towards the abandoned position. Wahed had become my role model.

A fighter jet roared above, and I was somewhat reassured. My heart pounded as I arrived at the position. What would I find? The position was enormous, like an abandoned fortress. I crossed to the west side and used the battlement to support my rifle as I looked through the scope. A little over half a mile away I could see the bridge ISIS had laid over the trench. A stream of vehicles and ISIS fighters crossed the line unhindered. There was no doubt. I could see it with my own eyes. The front had fallen.

Most of the enemy forces were heading north, towards Tel Skuf. But at least one vehicle and several ISIS fighters moved along the front line in my direction. They stopped to search one of the neighboring unit's many abandoned positions and I assumed I had a little time before they reached me. My mouth was bone dry. I found a bottle of water in the field kitchen and emptied it in a single gulp. Then I went to work.

I found a .50 caliber machine gun and several RPG-7 rocket-propelled grenade launchers. They could be useful. I prepared the weapons for firing, trying not to think about what would happen if reinforcements didn't arrive soon. Would they really let me fight alone?

Machine gun fire rattled abruptly from the position I had just left. Several short bursts followed. Was my unit also under attack? If so, I couldn't count on their help. It was not unthinkable that they too would flee, leaving me completely alone on the front. I readied my weapons and tried not to project. It was out of my control now.

I scouted westward toward the enemy heading straight for me. They were still too far away to engage with my rifle or the grenade launchers, so I tried the .50 caliber machine gun. It was broken. My plan had been pure madness but running back now was out of the question. Then I heard voices behind me.

"Come on, get in position! Hurry, they're coming!"

I was relieved beyond words. A handful of our soldiers quickly got into position and started shooting at the enemy.

"Fuck, don't shoot yet!" I shouted. "They're too far away. Wait until they get closer." More soldiers arrived. They lacked situational awareness, and chaos ensued. I shouted at the soldiers again to hold their fire. Karwan, my roommate, told me to retreat to our own position. I refused.

"Mike, we have to go back," He said. "Haji sent me to get you." I refused again. Karwan got out his phone and called Haji, who ordered me to return. I ended the conversation in anger. Why did I have to go back now? Were they afraid of losing me and having to explain to the general why they hadn't followed me?

Karwan called the unit's second in command, who also ordered me back. The enemy was almost within range, but if I disobeyed this order, I risked getting thrown out of the unit. Haji drove over and ordered Karwan and me into the truck. I was bitter, but a growing number of the fleeing soldiers had returned to the fight.

Back at our own position, the angry second in command waited. He told Haji to keep an eye on me before disappearing. Hirani walked over to me.

"Where's your PKM?" I asked the Swede. One of the officers had taken the machine gun, but he had gotten hold of an AK-47.

"One of our guys got shot in the head, so I got his rifle," he said, looking it over. "The stock is a bit loose, but it seems fine otherwise." I asked who had been killed but didn't recognize the name.

I sat down, angry about having been sent back. I turned my scope westward in time to witness an advancing vehicle get hit by a wire-guided anti-tank missile. Everyone cheered wildly as the sound of the explosion reached us. Karwan began shooting in the air. The skies were filled with Coalition aircraft and helicopters raining missiles and bombs on the

Islamists.

"Daesh has taken over Tel Skuf and driven all our forces out of the town," Hirani said. I was speechless. The attack had been successful, and obviously well planned. This explained the increased enemy activity during the previous weeks. They had done proper reconnaissance and prepared thoroughly.

Two American Black Hawk helicopters circled low above us. They were putting themselves at a great risk flying at such low altitude. When I saw the red cross painted on the sides, I realized they had come to evacuate wounded soldiers, but whose? They wouldn't risk getting shot down to evacuate local troops. An RPG-7 grenade exploded just in front of one helicopter and a cloud of black smoke hung in the air as the chopper rose to safety. Tracers flew by, and a grenade detonated in the air near the other helicopter. Karwan picked up his ringing phone.

"They say an American soldier was killed in action," Karwan said.

The half of our unit who had the week off had heard of the attack and headed straight for Tel Skuf. North of town, opposite us, they had joined a small group of American special forces entering Tel Skuf. They had received heavy incoming fire, and an American, thirty-one-year-old Charles Keating IV, had been killed. Another American was wounded.

"We must get into the town too," I said to Hirani. "There's no use waiting here." He agreed. Peshmerga forces had regained possession of the front line and were about to surround Tel Skuf, but the town itself was still under ISIS control. Hirani and I approached Marwan, one of the unit's veteran soldiers who had served in the PKK and had a lot of combat experience from Syria. He had severed relations with the guerillas for some reason and joined our unit.

"Should we get into the town before the party is over?" I asked Marwan. He was in. With Karwan driving one of the pickups, Hirani in back, Marwan on the mounted 14.5mm machine gun me in the passenger seat, we raced toward Tel Skuf.

Large convoys were headed for the town and I was reassured to see our troops had regained their courage. We passed a huge crater in the middle of the road next to a destroyed Peshmerga armored vehicle. We later learned that an ISIS suicide vehicle had taken the road toward our front to attack us from the rear. Two soldiers from another unit had spotted the vehicle, driven at full speed toward it and blocked the road, averting a catastrophe at great personal cost. The suicide bomber had been forced to blow his vehicle too early. Both our soldiers had survived, but judging from the wreckage, they must have been severely injured. They were heroes in my eyes.

A queue of military vehicles waited to enter Tel Skuf. Huge pillars of smoke rose from continuous air strikes and wrecked vehicles flew high in the air. I hoped the planes would take out most of the enemy vehicles, but I imagined countless ISIS fighters were barricaded in the buildings. We might have to fight our way from house to house.

Soldiers ahead of us in the queue started shooting at the nearest buildings. Soon everyone joined in. Marwan fired the 14.5mm machine gun and the pickup rocked from side to side.

"Shall I fire?" Karwan asked. I hadn't seen anything or heard incoming fire, but I gave him the thumbs up, so he could take part in the fun too. He pointed his rifle out the window and began shooting while I took over steering through the slowly moving queue. Traffic eventually stopped altogether.

I jumped out of the car and told Hirani to follow. My body craved combat. I didn't want to be one of the last ones into the town. There was shooting on all sides. Hirani and I ran forward. Three armored vehicles and a pickup with a mounted SPG-9 recoilless rifle led the queue.

"Hirani, let's follow these guys and use the cars as a shield," I said. He didn't object. I was impressed by the boy's courage. We entered town's outskirts with the first vehicles. The convoy slowly rolled forward, and we kept pace behind the armored vehicles with a handful of other soldiers, looking for the enemy. The convoy picked up speed and soon we were running as fast as we could to avoid being left behind.

"Slow the fuck down!" someone shouted.

Our strategy was not the best. Instead of taking the town one block at a time, the convoy drove straight to the town center, leaving us in the dust. It finally stopped at a crossroads under heavy fire and we caught up.

I knelt, panting, next to a stopped vehicle and assessed the situation. Intense enemy fire came from a building at the far end of one street. The pickup with the recoilless rifle entered the intersection to provide covering fire as enemy bullets flew over our heads. The guy on the SPG-9 took aim at the building, but the pickup, completely exposed, was shot to pieces. Before he could get a shot off, the guy on the SPG-9 and the driver threw themselves out of the vehicle and ran for cover behind a brick wall.

I emptied my magazine and pulled back into cover. ISIS' firepower was massive, and they were good. I couldn't spot them during the few seconds I fired at the building, but apparently, they could see us well. As our armored vehicles entered the crossroads, the enemy shredded their tires. The trucks backed up; they had taken a hell of a beating. As the vehicles retreated, hand grenades rained over us from the other side of the brick wall we had taken cover behind.

"Fuck, they are right behind here!" I shouted to Hirani. The grenades were homemade, with fuses that had to be lit. Luckily, they overshot their mark. I looked for ways over or around the wall as our vehicles and soldiers pulled out. If Hirani and I were left behind, the risk of dying by friendly fire was as great as the risk of being shot by the enemy.

"Hirani, let's get out of here," I yelled. Retreat left a bitter taste in my mouth but being shot by our own would taste worse. Driving straight into the town center, the hornet's nest, had been insane. That none of us had died was pure luck.

Hirani and I collapsed in a ditch along the road at the edge of town. We had fought for many hours and were exhausted and dehydrated.

"That was crazy," Hirani said. "Let's not do that again. We should find our guys." I agreed. It was risky fighting alongside people you didn't know, especially down here.

"Aren't you thirsty?" I asked Hirani.

"Brother, I'm dying here," the Swede laughed.

"I have an idea," I said. "Follow me."

We were two blocks from a small shop run by local soldiers where we often bought snacks and energy drinks. It was our next target. With rifles raised, we ran back into town. Bullets flew as we closed in on the shop and we barely managed to kick in the door and find cover. Hirani kept guard at the door and I grabbed several boxes of Wild Tiger and ice cream. We downed them in record time. Outside, the shooting and explosions continued unabated. We had just risked our lives for a drink.

"Definitely worth it," I said.

A few of our guys showed up after a while.

"What's up, Adel?" I asked. He said we were regrouping at our two houses in Tel Skuf, then we'd search the nearest blocks for the enemy. Adel emptied the refrigerator of soda and candy.

"Wahed is on his way," he added. "He took the first flight from Beirut to Erbil and will probably be here this evening." I was relieved. The guys could lack initiative without the general.

We left the shop and joined the rest of the unit at our houses. Saad lay on the lawn with a bandage around one foot. He had been wounded for the second time in two months.

"We came along the main road with the Americans when Daesh opened fire," he explained dejectedly. "An American was killed and I was hit by more shrapnel."

The houses were buzzing with activity. I found the officer responsible for ammunition storage.

"I need ammo for my M16," I said.

"What are you going to do with it?" he asked. I was astounded.

"We are about to search the town and I need to replenish what I've used!" We were in the middle of a major battle and I had to justify getting ammunition? Reluctantly he handed me some bullets.

As I refilled my magazines a crash sounded from the street. A drone had fallen from the sky and nearly hit Ayhan. He grabbed it and smashed the camera with a rock. On closer inspection, it wasn't one of the commercial drones ISIS used, but an expensive Israeli-made military drone that had to belong to the Coalition. It buzzed pathetically and flapped its wings like an injured bird. Could this day get any more surreal? I was about to get my answer.

17 BLOOD MAKES THE GRASS GROW

The enemy had taken over Tel Skuf in spectacular fashion. We were ordered to conduct a house to house search and began to clear neighborhoods on the outskirts of town. The most intense fighting was at the town center, but estimates had as many as three hundred ISIS fighters and fifty vehicles in the operation and we had to expect them everywhere. Hirani and I secured the roofs and covered our guys on the street as they searched the houses.

The first were empty, but it didn't take long before the Swede and I drew incoming fire. We took cover behind a brick wall. It was difficult to locate the gunfire's origin, so we stayed low, hoping the shooting would cease. A burst flew just above Hirani's head. I gaped at him. He looked back at me and broke into laughter. He was as crazy as I was. I had found my battle buddy.

A single projectile glanced off a satellite dish. We were probably getting fired at from a great distance if the bullet didn't penetrate. I crawled forward, picked up the projectile and gave it to Hirani.

"Here, a little souvenir."

The fire finally ceased and we raced down an outside staircase to rejoin the unit. The general was back, dressed in a beautifully tailored suit. He quickly added his combat vest and rifle.

"Okay, let's hunt down these bastards!" he shouted. Our spirits were high as we moved towards the town center to a symphony of explosions and shooting. The town had been demolished by air strikes and suicide vehicles.

We learned later that for the first time during the war against ISIS, Coalition aircraft had run out of bombs. The pilots had resorted to strafing, the risky tactic of flying in at low altitude and shooting with built-in machine guns. The Coalition sent almost all available fighter jets, bombers, close air support aircrafts, attack drones and helicopters. I had never before seen such a display over such a small area.

We rounded a corner toward gunfire from one of the main streets and saw two Peshmerga soldiers firing into an alley. With the general leading, we ran to their aid. Two ISIS fighters lay dead in the alley. That morning I had witnessed panic, fear and cowardice among my colleagues. Now, I witnessed bravery. The two Peshmerga had stood alone in the street not faltering under enemy fire.

Several men looted the corpses for weapons, ammunition and other valuables as Hirani and I moved down the street to search more houses. It was getting dark. We were about to enter a building when shooting and explosions erupted nearby. We ran to the scene. A dead ISIS fighter lay outside a house and part of a second-floor wall and the roof were blown away.

"What happened?" I asked one of the soldiers.

"A suicide bomber just blew himself up. He only killed himself," he said.

On the second-floor, another dead ISIS fighter lay with his legs jammed under part of the roof, which had collapsed when his friend exploded. His torso hung halfway down the outside wall, and a long stripe of blood streamed from his head to the ground. The general and Saad were removing magazines from the corpse.

I later saw a video of the incident. The trapped ISIS fighter had been alive when the general reached him and assured him he would receive medical treatment. The terrorist spat in his face, a gross insult in the Middle East. The general calmly wiped away the spit, pulled out his pistol and shot him in the head six times. The video was brutal, but neither surprised nor shocked me. Although the general had a big heart, his temperament was volatile. People walked on eggshells around him for this reason.

I couldn't condemn his actions. A life in this part of the world doesn't have the same value as a life in Norway. Death is an everyday part of life. The general had grown up surrounded by killing and violence and didn't know any other way. He was a product of the culture. I couldn't lecture locals about the Geneva Conventions or international law when it came to the treatment of ISIS fighters, who themselves engage in the most contemptable of executions the world has ever seen.

Night fell, and we declared our neighborhoods cleared. We passed countless corpses as we walked to the edge of town to find a ride to Baqofah. Body parts, entrails, pieces of flesh and bone shards littered the streets under a film of gray dust.

"Those two can't be more than fourteen or fifteen years old," Hirani said, clearly upset, as we walked by a pair of corpses. Child soldiers. A sure sign the enemy was getting desperate.

Back in Baqofah, we fell asleep to sporadic shooting from the neighboring town. We were filthy and hungry, but mostly we were exhausted. Hirani went to bed fully clothed. I called Susanne, told her about the day, without going into detail, and assured her the battle was over and I was okay. I told her how much I loved her, then fell asleep.

It wasn't more than two or three hours before the alarm sounded again. I jumped out of bed and dressed in a hurry. My entire body ached and my head pounded. My combat vest held four times more ammunition than the others' and I was one of only a few wearing heavy ballistic plates. I had carried all this weight for an entire day with little food or water. I felt like a truck had run me over the previous day. Mostly I felt like going back to sleep. Adrenaline came to my rescue, and soon enough I was ready for battle again. Hirani was so exhausted he could barely get out of bed.

"It's probably nothing Hirani," I assured him. "People are nervous. Someone probably thought they saw Daesh. You stay here and rest."

I grabbed my rifle and staggered to a waiting pickup truck. We headed for the front line behind the general's SUV. It was early. The sun had just risen and the chill air hitting my face woke me up fast. I had no idea where we were going or why. On our right flank, we approached the front line position our neighboring unit had abandoned the day before. Live fire confirmed this wasn't a false alarm.

The pickup screeched to a halt. I jumped out and found cover behind the hood. Gunfire rang out on all sides. Bullets flew overhead.

"Karwan, what's going on?" I shouted, adjusting my scope.

"Daesh is in the grass in front of us!"

Several ISIS fighters had escaped from Tel Skuf during the night and headed back to Batnaya. Our neighboring unit had spotted them. They were boxed in by two of our positions and two armored vehicles that had come in from the rear. We pulled up behind a hillock where soldiers from the two units gathered. I rolled onto the mound and looked through my scope. Islamist fire came from a grassy area no larger than a football pitch. We couldn't see anything. Our soldiers shot randomly into the tall grass.

"This isn't working!" the general shouted. "We have to advance and take them out one by one!"

As in Aski Moskul, the general took control even though it wasn't our show. He ordered an armored vehicle with a top cover armed with a rooftop PKM to ease forward. Using the vehicle as cover, the general, two officers from the neighboring unit and I advanced with covering fire from the mound.

"This is crazy," I thought.

As we approached the enemy, incoming fire intensified. The top cover fired burst after burst into the tall grass. I crouched to the left of the hood and fired at targets I couldn't see. Hand grenades rained down on us. We were getting close. A grenade landed just in front of the vehicle. I knelt behind the wheel as it exploded three yards away. Black smoke and dirt filled the air. I jumped up and emptied my magazine at the grenade's source. The situation seemed hopeless. More grenades fell and the vehicle was peppered with bullets. The enemy was invisible.

"Back up the vehicle! Back, back, back!" the general shouted.

We retreated a few yards and the general changed his mind. He took over as top cover and ordered full speed ahead. I walked by the vehicle's side using the hood as a shield. An enemy jumped from the grass and sprinted toward the front line, fifty or sixty yards away. I caught him in my sights and squeezed the trigger. He fell. I felt nothing. No remorse, joy, fear or anger. It was like being back at the Camp Rena shooting range. My senses were heightened, my mind focused on hitting the target. Nothing more.

Another ISIS fighter attempted the front line. I made out his features clearly through my scope. He was older, with a long, white beard and a big belly. Halfway up the berm he fell in hail of bullets.

"Stop shooting, stop shooting!" the general shouted as the man collapsed. I fired three more bullets into his back.

Better safe than sorry," I thought.

Enemy fire slackened and we slowly advanced. An explosion erupted in front of me. A body shot into the air, arms and legs everywhere. Bits of flesh and organs rained down. What had just happened? The guys cheered.

"He blew himself up!" the general shouted from the roof.

We continued our advance. Another suicide bomber exploded. I fell to the ground under a hail of body parts. We reached the front line and waited for reinforcements from the rear. One of our soldiers ran straight up the berm and fired down the other side. I ran toward the berm and sank up to my chest in a mudhole. The general and another soldier got trapped behind me. I held my rifle high and tried to wriggle loose. An officer from the other unit grabbed my arm. He pulled as I crawled through the mud, speckled with bits of the suicide bombers.   Eventually we all emerged, completely covered in mud.

The field was quiet and littered with bodies, many shot through the head at close range. It was unlikely any were still alive. The green grass was stained red with blood. Looting had begun. Behind me, a corpse burned, the smoke blowing straight into my face. The older ISIS fighter I'd shot lay on the berm. One of our soldiers stood over his corpse hurling insults at his female relatives. Many of the dead wore bandages from the previous day's battle. I tried counting our kills, but numerous bodies were blown to pieces. It was impossible not to step on what, just an hour earlier, had been part of a living, breathing human being. We had killed about twenty ISIS fighters without losing a single man.

Next to a headless corpse, Karwan and another guy from our unit inspected a large pile of rifles they had salvaged. Karwan grinned when he saw me and showed off the cache.

"Look here, Mike," he said proudly. "These belonged to Daesh."

A group of soldiers surrounded the general, who was on the radio with the commander of the enemy we had just decimated. The commander was a Kurd and the conversation was lively.

"Wahed, one of them is alive!" a soldier behind me shouted. The general shouted back that no one was to harm him. The ISIS fighter was unconscious, face turned in the mud, entrails protruding from under him. When I had passed him earlier I thought him dead. Perhaps he was lying on someone else's guts. With the ISIS commander on the radio, the general slowly walked over.

"You are no Kurd. You're a dog, you hear me? A dog!" the general snapped. He turned the body over and removed the magazines. Soldiers continued the looting. The young, long-haired ISIS fighter moved.

"He's alive. Allahu akbar," a soldier shouted.

"Allahu akbar! Allahu akbar," others repeated, mocking him. The young man had been shot in the thigh. He moaned in pain.

"Bandage his leg," the general commanded, then informed the ISIS-commander we had one of his men alive. I knelt next to the man and cut open his pants with my scissors. He had been shot several times. Could I have hit him? The general assured the ISIS commander we would take good care of the prisoner and provide him with medical treatment.

"I don't care. You can kill him for all I care," the commander retorted.

The general handed his radio to the prisoner. Abu Eshaq was a nineteen-year-old from Mosul. He apologized to his commander for having been captured. I bandaged his thigh and reflected on his commander's complete lack of empathy for his own men.

Another explosion rocked us. Nearby, a second unconscious Islamist had come to, and blown himself to Kingdom Come. I realized how reckless we had been. From now on I would make sure all bodies were actually dead by giving them a headshot.

In the chaos after the explosion, one of our soldiers started kicking Abu Eshaq. The general restrained him.

"No one is to abuse the prisoner!" the general ordered. "Drive him to the field hospital!"

I didn't trust the guys to follow that order, so I went along. We loaded the prisoner in the back of a pickup truck and headed for the field hospital in Tel Skuf. We were stopped several times by soldiers wanting to view him. At times I had to physically prevent them from beating the young man.

"Drive on, for fuck's sake! Why are you stopping?" I shouted to the driver. Although I hated ISIS and everything it represented, I pitied the pathetic creature curled up at my feet.

We got out on the road and picked up the pace. The man next to me stepped on the prisoner, who squirmed in pain. Abu Eshaq looked at me in despair while his tormenter laughed. The same man had had no less than three unintentional discharges the day before, one of them right next to my foot. My patience with him ran out.

"That's enough!" I shouted. "Did you hear what Wahed said? This is the last time you touch the prisoner!" He removed his foot and spat in the prisoner's face.

The field hospital had been demolished in the previous day's bombing and only two nurses remained. They looked bewildered when we deliver an enemy patient.

"Come here, take him," Karwan said. One of the nurses seemed terrified.

"Are you going to execute him?" the nurse asked.

"No, Wahed wants you to patch him up," he explained.

They placed the prisoner on a blanket outside the ruined hospital. I sat in a chair nearby to collect my thoughts. Before long the nurses called me.

"We need some help here," one said. "Can you cut away his clothes with your scissors, including his underwear?" I removed his clothes and covered his groin with a blanket.

"Since you're already at it, can you do the rest too?" They seemed afraid to touch him. I removed my earlier bandage, cleaned the wounds and applied new dressings. The young man was clearly in pain but also appeared drugged. While ISIS amputated the fingers of tobacco smokers, they had no problem using harder drugs themselves, either to enhance battle performance or to dull pain.

Back in Baqofah, Hirani was up and about.

"What in the world?" he asked.

I was covered in mud and blood. I took off my gear and noticed a long stripe of blood along my hearing protection under a bone shard attached to a piece of flesh. On my vest I found several more small pieces of the suicide bombers. I showered at the general's house, looking at two small birds sitting outside the frosted window. They sang without worry, ignorant of today's events. I thought about the green grass turned red. In some places it had looked airbrushed with blood.

American soldiers have an expression that blood makes the grass grow. It was truer here, on the Nineveh plains where civilization had begun thousands of years ago, than anywhere else. Countless wars had fertilized these plains. This day wasn't extraordinary. This was how life was here; how it had been for millennia. Why would it be different in the future? There were still places in the world where natural order ruled. Where survival belonged to the fittest. Today, we happened to be the fittest.

18 WAR AND LOVE

The period following the battle for Tel Skuf was almost as hard as the combat itself. The first days, we searched the town, finding mostly corpses and undetonated suicide vehicles. ISIS had reinforced civilian cars, tractors and bulldozers with thick steel plates, and mounted machine guns and recoilless rifles filled with explosives. It was straight out of a Mad Max movie. It didn't take long for local forces to start fighting over vehicles.

Our unit's infrastructure had completely broken down. In Baqofah we were out of food and water. It was a triumphant moment when I found a lunch pack in the rucksack of a dead enemy. I sat down next to the corpse and inhaled juice boxes, salted peanuts and dates before continuing my search of bombed-out buildings.

Having exhausted my ammunition in battle, I replenished my supply from dead ISIS fighters. Many rounds were covered in dried blood and some had bullet holes in them. After washing them and discarding damaged ammunition, I had enough to refill my stores.

My equipment had taken a beating and my pistol's front sight had fallen off. I risked contacting my Rena team leader, who was in Erbil with the Norwegian Armed Forces.

"Would it be possible for your armorer to fix a new sight for me?" I asked. "Perhaps he could look at my rifle too." Back in Norway, armorers thoroughly checked all weapons every third month. It gave a sense of security I didn't have at the front, where I fought with an old rifle bought on the black market. My team leader seemed happy to hear from me and promised to do what he could to help.

We had lost one man in battle and several more had been wounded. Many resigned because of the terrible conditions and unpaid wages. We had never been so undermanned, and we legitimately feared our unit would be disbanded.

For weeks after Tel Skuf, Hirani and I didn't get a single night's continuous sleep. We took shifts outside our hours or at the front, day and night, and were on constant high alert. Our troops were paranoid. Rumors circulated about suspicious people in the area and many worried about enemy fighters behind our lines. We hunted for them almost daily. We never found anyone.

Early one morning an agitated Karwan shook me awake; I hadn't slept more than an hour. I dressed in a hurry without question. Getting yanked out of sleep had become standard and I no longer cared about the reason.

"Hirani doesn't have to come, but bring your laptop and hurry!" Karwan said. I ran after him with my rifle in one hand and laptop in the other. When we reached Tel Skuf, we parked outside our neighboring unit's headquarters.

"Hurry, Wahed is waiting for you," Karwan said. He stayed with the car. Inside, the general sat with the neighboring unit's commander and a group of high ranking officers.

"Mike, come here!" the general growled. "Show Tariq how his men fled from the front line."

I sat down next to General Tariq and played my helmet camera footage documenting hundreds of his soldiers fleeing and me running to cover his unit's position. Tariq shook his head in shock; the atmosphere was tense. His officers had flat out denied fleeing. When they saw the video, they hurriedly claimed it was a tactical retreat. General Wahed was incensed. I was uncomfortable, having caught the officers in their lie. Although Tariq commanded several thousand men to our one hundred and fifty, no one dared challenge Wahed. A past as a hitman had its benefits. After cursing the officers, Wahed stood and stormed out of the room.

A steady stream of journalists arrived at the front to report on the fight for Tel Skuf. The battle was getting international attention, probably because an American special forces operator had been killed. Saad's video had captured Americans in combat. The Guardian newspaper bought it and the footage went viral. My video of dead ISIS fighters sprawled in the bloody grass was a hit on Instagram and I gained many new followers, including Coalition soldiers.

I had previously received messages from Dutch soldiers working with the Telemark Battalion in Northern Iraq. They sent pictures posing with my old colleagues, which I found entertaining. Norwegian leadership would probably not be as amused. The Dutch told me a small Norwegian team was part of the large Coalition presence near the Mosul Dam, which surprised me after Norwegian leadership's reticence to provide combat support.

Through other sources I confirmed the Norwegian team had moved to the dam after little success training local forces in Erbil and the small town of Chamchamal. Not unexpectedly, leadership back home rejected the move and ordered the team back to the safety of Erbil, I guessed because of "Mosul" in the dam's name, rather than actual security conditions. The dam was safe enough for other Coalition countries, I thought.

I received messages from American soldiers who had been in the Tel Skuf battle. A crew member from one of the Black Hawk helicopters reported finding several bullet holes in the helicopter's hull, in addition to being fired on by the RPG-7 grenades I had witnessed. I also heard from Louis, who had been working for a private security firm in Afghanistan since leaving our front the previous year.

"I was glued to the screen between shifts at our base and constantly checked Instagram for updates from you and Hirani," Louis told me. He earned good money in Afghanistan but seeing his former front fall upset him greatly. Instead of going home for his first leave, he went straight to Erbil. A couple weeks after the attack, to my great joy, he was back at our front. Many probably thought breaking his lucrative contract with the security firm was madness, but I understood and respected his decision.

Dwekh Nawsha had hosted a handful of Western volunteers in Baqofah before Louis returned, but most stayed for only a couple weeks. I trusted Louis, and when he returned I decided it was time for a change. I got the general's permission to bring the Western volunteers - from the US, the UK, France, Poland and even South Korea - to the front line.

I found a guard post for the Westerners and arranged transportation to the front every night with my team. The Assyrians still weren't interested in helping. Here we were, defending their villages and towns, and they were nowhere to be seen on the front line. Dwekh Nawsha never failed to disappoint me. During the battle of Tel Skuf, several Western Dwekh Nawsha volunteers, including American Chance, had tried to assist us and the Assyrians physically stopped them from leaving Baqofah. Chance was understandably bitter.

When Louis returned, the Western volunteers decided to test fire their rifles. I brought them to a small field behind the village where we could shoot undisturbed. Chance fired ten or twelve shots before having an apparent malfunction. On closer inspection, we discovered the rest of his magazine was filled with empty cartridges! Local Assyrians had switched out the live rounds to avoid buying ammunition for themselves. It could have cost Chance his life in battle. What self-centered assholes some of the Dwekh Nawsha were!

I felt sorry for Louis and the others who had to live with those people, but I was thankful for the Western volunteers' support at the front. After months on high alert, Hirani and I were exhausted, mentally and physically. With Louis back, we could finally let our guard down and get away from the front. I bought a ticket to Norway and sent Hirani back to his mother in Sulaymaniyah. I looked forward to leaving but, as always, felt bad doing so. It was reassuring to know Louis would watch over things in our absence.

Shortly after Hirani left, the house and warehouse on the front line were attacked by unseen enemy with a recoilless rifle hidden in no man's land. Three projectiles hit us and seven of our men were injured, one gravely. He lost nearly half his face when a shell penetrated the outer wall and two interior walls. It would have been more merciful had he died instantly.

Just before I left Baqofah, an unexpected visitor arrived from Erbil. My old Camp Rena team leader had replied that the Norwegian forces couldn't repair my weapons. I wasn't surprised. So I had turned to Instagram and quickly received more than 200 offers to send a new sight for my pistol or to help me buy one cheaply. A Frenchman from an Erbil-based humanitarian aid organization offered to send a brand-new sight with his assistant Noel and a Kurdish security service escort. It didn't exactly seem like humanitarian aid, but I accepted.

Several days later, the young Frenchman, armed with his own Glock pistol, arrived with a security service officer. After mounting the new sight, I showed Noel around the village, ending at the church, where he fell to his knees and prayed. He was very interested in the area and I suspected his organization wanted to rebuild ruined Christian villages as soon as the situation allowed. I thanked him and promised to keep his boss updated on conditions in our area.

After saying goodbye to the guys in Baqofah, I spent a couple days in a hotel in Erbil. It had been two intense and exhausting months, and I needed to unwind and collect my thoughts before going back home, now more than ever.

The hardest part of life at the front was not the atrocities I witnessed or living in constant danger. Even the terrible living conditions paled next to knowing what I was putting those back home through, especially Susanne.

When I first met Susanne, she struck me as a confident and independent girl, very mature for her age. Later, I discovered a hidden vulnerability that awoke something in me. When I fell for Susanne, there was no turning back.

Perhaps there were underlying issues, but until Susanne, I had been afraid of commitment and didn't want anyone emotionally dependent on me. I reasoned it would complicate the lifestyle I sought. Now I wanted nothing more than to protect, care for and love her. That was tougher than either of us had imagined. The geographic distance between us and the constant threat to my life took a tremendous toll on our relationship. Susanne had countless dreams of me returning home in a coffin.

"After your funeral I went back to your apartment to collect my things, but I just lay on the bed crying," she said. "I know it was just a dream, but it felt so real."

I didn't fear death, but I feared how Susanne would deal with mine. Our relationship struggled. Several times I thought it was over, but Susanne managed to keep the promise engraved on the dogtag she'd given me before I first left. We texted each other whenever possible during the day. At night I found someplace I could be alone, usually on the roof, and called her. Our conversations could last for hours. I loved listening to her talk about her day, her studies and her cat, Bianchi. Hearing about her everyday life in Norway made me forget where I was for a brief moment.

I avoided talking about the front line. She didn't like being reminded I was fighting in a war. Instead I talked about our dogs and what we had eaten. It wasn't unusual for her to hear shooting from the front line, or grenades as they struck around our house.

"What was that?" she would ask.

"Nothing. It was just a grenade impact, but it's fine," I would reassure her. "They never hit their targets anyway." I minimized the danger, but I'm not sure she believed me.

We would talk until she dozed off. I stayed on the line until she was sound asleep, or else she would wake from my hanging up, call back and scold me. I thought it was cute. She didn't like going to bed without me, so I stayed with her over the phone. I loved hearing her breathe as she slept. I could listen for half an hour or more. I got a lot of shit from the guys, especially Hirani, for being unsociable, but I could not have cared less.

When Susanne and I were finally reunited, our first hug was always a very long one. Neither of us said anything. We would just held each other in deep silence. Only the two of us existed and nothing else mattered.

I always brought Susanne a souvenir. This time it was a teddy bear I had found in a demolished house in Tel Skuf. I thought it would fit well into her collection of stuffed animals. So did she.

I had only a couple of weeks at home and I spent it almost entirely with Susanne. We went to Berlin on our first vacation in more than two years. On July 14, we checked into a nice hotel and Susanne showed me all her favorite places in the city. In the evening we swam in the hotel pool before going to our room. I turned on CNN. It was Bastille Day, France's national holiday. A news alert at the bottom of the screen announced another terrorist attack in France, this time in Nice. A truck had driven into a large crowd celebrating the holiday, killing and injuring many.

Leaders around the world, including ours, were quick to condemn the attack, but no one grabbed the bull by the horns. No one said what I was thinking: Radical Islam is our enemy and must be conquered by any means necessary. The attack motivated me to continue my fight against the caliphate.

Back in Norway, I prepared for what I hoped would be my last trip to Northern Iraq. Everything was in place for the Mosul offensive to begin that fall. I was prepared to remain until the city was conquered, even if it meant a longer stay this time.

Susanne would soon serve her conscription in the Norwegian Armed Forces. I hoped that would make it easier for me to stay in Iraq until the goal was achieved. I took her to the stores where I usually bought equipment. With money donated through Instagram, I got a new combat vest and uniform. I bought the same commercial drone ISIS used to donate to the unit. If ISIS could map out our front, we could do the same to theirs.

From home, I followed my unit's area closely and received weekly updates from Louis. Chance and several other Dwekh Nawsha volunteers had left, but a couple new guys filled some of the spots. Louis posted an Instagram video of himself and a new American named John being narrowly missed by mortar grenade shrapnel at the front. The shockwave knocked them both over and they laughed and seemed fine. But Louis admitted to me that he struggled with headaches and dizziness following the explosion. It was a vivid reminder of what I was returning to.

My time with Susanne was nearing its end. I was leaving for Erbil and she would leave for Northern Norway at the beginning of August. Before I left I gave her the keys to my apartment. It was a big step for me, but it felt very right.

19 EYES ON MOSUL

It had become almost routine for Erbil airport guards to confiscate my equipment, a situation I usually cleared up with a few phone calls. But this time, rules had been tightened and more than $3,000 worth of gear was impounded, much-needed equipment for my unit - including the drone - made possible by Instagram followers. It was infuriating, especially since I planned to map out the neighboring town using the drone.

In Erbil I called all my contacts, including Agit, the president's nephew, but the new head of airport security would not bend the rules. I was bitter that bureaucracy would hinder me from helping its own country and my unit, which sorely lacked government support.

Before my leave, I had begun coordinating a project with Global Surgical and Medical Support Group, or GSMSG, an American aid organization that sends volunteer surgeons and doctors to assist hospitals in the Kurdish Region. The previous year, I had been approached for support by its head, an American named Aaron. I had met Aaron in Sulaymaniyah a few months earlier when visiting Eivind, and he had impressed me. I had promoted GSMSG on Instagram and the group quickly gained followers, many of whom donated money, medical supplies and equipment or offered to volunteer.

While I was in Norway, Aaron and I had recruited a team of Western military veterans with medical backgrounds to spend three weeks at my front training local forces in first aid. I had long been concerned about my fellow soldiers' inadequate medical knowledge. I knew that if I was injured at the front, I couldn't count on even basic treatment from those around me.

I met the GSMSG team at the market in Erbil, where they were shopping for uniforms and equipment for the upcoming medical mission.

"Long time no see!" a familiar voice exclaimed. Nick had worked in my Telemark Battalion squadron but had recently quit his job at Rena and joined GSMSG.

"Welcome to Kurdistan, Buddy!" I replied with a hug. Two other Norwegians, Max-Hendrik and Ola, had also been in the Norwegian armed forces. The rest of the team was comprised of Americans, Canadians, Brits and an Australian. They seemed like a solid bunch.

After advising them on their purchases, we went to Ankawa, the Christian district, where we would spend the night before heading to the front. Eivind had come to visit from Kirkuk. We chatted with Nick, who confirmed what many others had told me.

"There was a lot of talk at Rena when your whereabouts became known," he said. "Leadership wasn't happy with your choice. Some in the unit shake their heads at what you and Eivind do down here, but it's envy for the most part."

Eivind had recently, by pure chance, encountered a group of former Telemark Battalion colleagues in Erbil.

"I was in a pickup going to shop in Erbil with local guys from my unit," he said. "We passed a convoy of armored SUVs that I recognized from when I was here with the armed forces. I got my driver to stop in the middle of traffic, jumped out and stopped the entire Norwegian procession.

"I ran to the nearest car and tore the door open. The guys were shocked at being stopped like that, and even more so seeing me in a Peshmerga uniform." I had to laugh.

"They weren't so talkative and referred me to their officers," he continued. "I told them they had broken their rules of engagement when they didn't shoot me as I opened the door." It was typical Eivind.

The next day Hirani arrived by cab from Sulaymaniyah, Eivind returned to his front and the Scandinavian group, and we headed for our front in a minibus with the GSMSG volunteers.

Along the way, several team members mentioned they had learned about GSMSG through my Instagram account and had volunteered because of my endorsement. At this point I had more than 150,000 followers, and it dawned on me just how much influence I had on social media. Here I had motivated people from three different continents to travel to a war zone and risk their lives to support the fight against ISIS.

I settled the team at the new field hospital outside Tel Skuf. Many local soldiers were interested in learning first aid and during the next three weeks, men from several units attended GSMSG classes. I also invited our neighboring unit, in an effort to improve relations after the meeting between Wahed and their officers earlier that summer.

Everyone who passed the courses received a diploma and a first aid kit, a big deal for the otherwise poorly equipped soldiers. GSMSG and their female team leader had done a fantastic job. General Tariq from the neighboring unit was so grateful he invited the group back. Even I felt somewhat safer. Many of my guys now knew basic first aid, and I could tell Aaron the mission had been a success.

It was September, and the Mosul offensive was fast approaching. ISIS was on the defensive in Iraq. Important cities such as Ramadi and Fallujah had been reclaimed by the Iraqis, who were fighting with revitalized spirit despite heavy losses. They slowly worked their way north towards Mosul, while Kurdish forces held the front in the north and east and awaited orders to advance. An undefended corridor to Syria lay to the west with the hope ISIS fighters would flee Iraq in that direction, much to the Syrian regime's great frustration.

The Coalition stepped up its efforts; the U.S. increased its ground forces to support the locals and I had to wonder why this hadn't happened earlier. The Coalition dropped pamphlets in Arabic over our front informing civilians of the coming offensive. As we watched through binoculars, the enemy in the neighboring town began digging trenches and laying out roadside bombs.

Kurdish and Iraqi leaders argued over the Peshmerga's role in the coming offensive. The Iraqis didn't want us inside Mosul, but rather, helping to take nearby towns and villages. Everyone knew Mosul would be a bloodbath, and I was convinced the Iraqis would have some common sense and ask for our assistance. I hadn't given up on my dream of taking part in the city's liberation, and I wasn't alone in that. Mosul was first prize for the few remaining Western volunteers. Most had either left by choice or been forced out after a series of unfortunate episodes. The largest remaining group of Western volunteers was stationed with Dwekh Nawsha at our front.

I was happy to see that Scottish James was back. He, Hirani, Louis, John and I quickly bonded. John had spent several months in another Peshmerga unit and had appeared frequently on local television. He was in his mid-twenties and over seven feet tall, quite a curiosity for the diminutive Kurds. When we shopped in Duhok, we could barely move ten yards without someone stopping us for a picture with John. I found it amusing, but James and Louis weren't thrilled with John's magnetism. But he was a good guy, and often visited our house with Louis. I asked John why he had left his old unit.

"There were several Westerners in my unit," he explained. "We were all thrown out after an American and a Romanian guy fucked it up." He took a drag on his cigarette.

"These two morons were bored, so one day while the Iraqis were engaged in an offensive nearby, they crossed the front line and ran into the nearest ISIS-controlled village. The Kurds thought they were joining ISIS, so they arrested all the Westerners." I thought I had misheard him.

"They did what?" Louis, who had heard the story before, chuckled.

"They ran into the nearest ISIS-controlled village during an ongoing offensive," John repeated. "They hid in the second floor of an empty house and entertained themselves by watching "Black Hawk Down" twice on their laptop 'til the fighting died down.

"The next day an ISIS fighter entered the house, inspected the first floor and left. The idiots were convinced they'd been discovered, so they ran onto the roof and started shooting at the dude. He got away and the guys escaped before he could return with reinforcements." I had heard many crazy stories about Western volunteers, but this was perhaps the worst.

"They were almost shot by the Kurds as they ran back to the front line," John said. "The Kurds no longer trusted us, so we were all sent away. I wasn't ready to go home, so Dwekh Nawsha became my solution."

We talked a lot about Mosul. Although the Assyrians in Dwekh Nawsha refused to participate in offensive action, we hoped James, John, and Louis could assist our unit. They had supported us on the front line throughout the summer and the general valued them. We hoped he would repay their efforts by letting them fight with us when the offensive started. They had earned it.

Not long after the GSMSG volunteers left I had another visitor from Erbil. Italian Alex, who the previous year had sought my support for building a tactical training center, planned to spend a couple weeks at our front.

During one of my visits to Erbil, I had inspected the center's impressive construction. Agit had secured some serious investors and, while the center wasn't finished, I could see it was going to be amazing. After a tour and shooting at one of the ranges, Alex and I had gone into his office. He had looked at me gravely.

"Now that the Mosul offensive is in sight, the Coalition is very interested in activity at your front," he had said. "I provide intelligence for the Italian forces at times. I'd like to visit you for a couple of weeks to give them a better understanding of the situation north of Mosul."

I hadn't been surprised to learn that Alex worked with the Italians. The Coalition's movements in Iraq were restricted, and it wasn't unusual for them to use Western citizens covertly for intelligence. Louis had a similar deal with American intelligence.

I respected Alex and he struck me as committed and professional. He had been among the first Westerners to join the Peshmerga and had quickly gained the Kurd's trust and esteem. The previous year he had built up and trained an elite force in Kirkuk, and he had fought ISIS several times. I had readily agreed to his plan.

"We'll say you want to spend a few weeks training our unit," I had suggested.

The general was gone so I had quite a lot of freedom. With Alex in Baqofah under the guise of instructor, we prepared for his clandestine mission. I gave him a tour of the front line, then we established an operations room on the second floor of our house. We scavenged whiteboards, office furniture and cabinets from the village school and set up Alex's laptops and radios.

We developed protocols and a communications system. James, John, and Louis reported their observations from the front line to Alex, Hirani or me staffing the operations room around the clock. We created a detailed record of the enemy's actions, Coalition bombings and the results. We sent daily reports to the Italians and to US intelligence through Louis. Occasionally we found time to shop for pasta, sauce and canned tuna in Hatarah, which Alex transformed into an authentic Italian meal, more or less. We were doing an important job, and things were going well, until one of the guys woke me one morning.

"Mike, you have visitors," he said. I dressed and went outside. I recognized the French special forces soldiers and knew it meant trouble. After the terrorist attack in Paris the previous year, the French had been very active at our front. Periodically they would establish themselves in our house and spend a few days sending up drones and calling in air strikes on ISIS. As almost no one in our unit spoke English, Hirani and I often interpreted for the French and the locals. We had gotten to know a few French soldiers well including their leader, who now stood outside our house with his unit. We shook hands.

"Good morning," he said, smiling. "We thought we'd spend a few days on your second floor and roof." I froze. It had been a long time since they had been here, and I hadn't expected them back during Alex's stay.

"Eh, second floor?" I said, as I scrambled mentally for an escape. "We have someone living there right now." His smile disappeared. The Kurdish intelligence service officer who accompanied them broke into the conversation.

"What did you say?" he demanded. "There's someone living up there? Who?" He eyed me suspiciously.

"Just a friend of mine who's helping us train," I began. Before I could explain further, the officer bolted up the stairs with his men on his heels. They burst in on Alex, asleep in the operations room.

The intelligence officer and the French were astonished by the maps, the array of equipment and weapons and the whiteboard lists of coordinates, radio frequencies and descriptions of events.

"What is going on here and who is he?" the intelligence officer shouted.

Alex had no documents to explain his presence at our front. He couldn't divulge he worked for the Italians and his vague answers angered the intelligence officer, who accused Alex of being a spy.

I feared Alex would be arrested so I called Samad, Agit's bodyguard. He didn't answer. The situation was getting tense. The officer started calling people too. Would the security service appear at any moment to pick up Alex? I tried Samad repeatedly, with no luck. The French, on the other hand, remained calm. They studied the whiteboards and seemed impressed by our work.

Alex finally admitted who he was working for and asked the French to call the Italian headquarters in Erbil to confirm his story. The French called, but the Italians denied any acquaintance with Alex.

"He's lying. Tell me who he really is!" the intelligence officer roared. Samad finally answered his phone. Samad wasn't only Agit's bodyguard, but a trusted man of the Barzani family, which gave him authority.

"Here, it's for you." I handed my phone politely to the intelligence officer, who was about to explode. Samad had gotten me out of sticky situations before, and I hoped he could save my skin again.

"Okay, he can stay," the intelligence officer said curtly, returning my phone. Alex was safe, for now. We explained our mission to the French leader and he agreed we should continue our work. The French were interested in the information we had gathered, and we didn't mind sharing.

The soldiers made camp in our house. There were more of them than last time and they seemed more focused. They mounted surveillance equipment and radio and satellite antennas on the roof, set up several computers in the operations room and sent up drones to surveil the area south of us. As one of their drones flew over an area outside Mosul the live feed disappeared. This was highly unusual and caused great concern.

"It's suspicious," a Frenchman named Jacques said. "Our Canadian colleagues experienced the same thing over the same area. They even lost a drone." The French guessed the radio signal was being jammed. Jacques didn't believe ISIS was capable of electronic warfare.

Who could be behind this then? Officers from the infamous Iranian Revolutionary Guard were in Iraq supporting the Iraqi army and the Shiite militia fighting ISIS. Could they be testing their electronic warfare capacity against Coalition forces?

We developed good relationships with the French, especially Jacques, one of the English speakers. Hirani and I entertained them with our combat videos on my laptop. They shared their field rations and cooked delicious ratatouille for dinner with vegetables purchased in Hatarah. We rarely ate as well as when the French visited.

The good times ended one day in early October. I was on guard outside the neighboring house when several French soldiers sprinted out of our house, jumped into their SUVs and raced off at full speed.

"Some of our guys were hit by a mortar grenade," Jacques yelled as he left.

Two hours later they returned, clearly distraught, especially Jacques. His uniform was covered with blood. I asked what had happened and he broke into tears.

The story slowly emerged. ISIS had intentionally crashed a drone behind our lines. Two local soldiers had retrieved it and brought it to the French. The drone's camera must have been active, because as soon as the French picked it up, a bomb detonated. Both locals were killed, and two French were severely injured. One lost both legs and was badly burned. The other lost a foot and also suffered horrible burns. Their leader said they would make it, but Hirani and I ached for Jacques. The French were our brothers in arms, it was as if our own men had been injured.

Attacks had increased while the French were with us. After the drone incident, they hastily packed their gear and withdrew indefinitely. Our front was no longer deemed safe for foreign forces. Hirani and I tore the shoulder patches from our uniforms and gave them to Jacques and another soldier. We hugged them hard.

"We'll cross the front line and drive south very soon. Then we will avenge your guys," I promised Jacques.

Not long after, Alex returned to Erbil and John and a couple other Westerner volunteers quit Dwekh Nawsha. James and Louis were, like me, dead set on taking part in the Mosul offensive. Although the date wasn't set, we knew it wouldn't be too long now.

An Iraqi brigade of several thousand men set up camp at Tel Skuf, with hundreds of armored vehicles, tanks and artillery guns. They couldn't sustain themselves there for long, so we knew the offensive was only a couple of weeks away, at most.

The brigade was Shiite, bad news for Mosul's mainly Sunni population. Shiites constitute more than sixty percent of Iraq's population. The Shiite units and militias had committed heinous war crimes against Sunni Muslims, who comprise about twenty percent.

The conflict between the two sects is almost as old as Islam itself, but in Iraq, the last decades had been especially bloody. Under Saddam Hussein, Iraq had been controlled by the Sunni minority, who had committed major atrocities against both Shiites and Kurds. After the 2003 American invasion, Sunni Muslims lost power and Shiites retaliated. This climate laid the foundation for radical Sunni Muslim groups such as ISIS.

Despite ISIS' extreme brutality, many Sunni Muslims supported the terrorists. Some thought ISIS a welcome alternative to the Shiite regime. Others may have believed they had no choice but to support the jihadists if they wanted to live. Whatever the reason, they would pay a high price when the Shiites marched into Mosul.

While Iraqi soldiers poured into Tel Skuf and anticipation mounted, I had to take a short trip to Erbil. The Norwegian Broadcasting Corporation, or NRK, had sent a well-known correspondent to Iraq and I had agreed to meet her.

Hirani and I took a cab to Erbil to meet Eivind and Knut at a café before they returned to Norway. Karl Håkon had gone home a few weeks earlier and the Scandinavian group had disbanded. Although I had urged them to be selective in admitting new members, they had accepted almost every Scandinavian who made it to Erbil on their own.

The first was a Swedish career criminal missing one eye and six fingers. He was so mentally unstable the team had feared he would hurt himself or others. After a short time, he had been driven back to Erbil and asked to leave the country. Another Swede had a Nazi past. Out of boredom, He and a Finn would fire guns indoors or expose themselves to local female soldiers. I wasn't surprised the group had disintegrated.

Given the circumstances, Eivind and Knut had done an excellent job and I was proud of them. Now they were leaving for good; but first we would spend the night celebrating Hirani's twentieth birthday.

The NRK correspondent eventually showed up with a cameraman and interpreter. Hirani suggested going to his aunt's house, where we could talk in peace. On the way Susanne called.

She had served two months of her Army conscription after training diligently for more than a year. She had beaten her entire military session group - including the men - on the physical tests and had been enjoying herself. She was even considering further service after conscription. She sounded tense.

"I was called to a meeting with the platoon leader and the intelligence and security officer today," she said. "They found out we're together and said I might lose my security clearance. They said you could pose a security risk since they're sending forces to Northern Iraq in a few months." I was stunned.

The car pulled up outside Hirani's aunt's house and the guys went inside. I stayed on the street, completely shocked. So the Norwegian Armed Forces still saw me as a security risk? I had offered the FSA and Norwegian intelligence my full support the year before, and for free! I had notified Norwegian forces in Erbil about the drone attack on the French, the first of its kind, in case they encountered similar tactics! Despite my assistance, I was considered a threat and Susanne, an innocent third party, might be thrown out of the forces?

"How did they find out?" I asked.

"Yesterday I talked to the chaplain in strict confidence about challenges in our relationship," she said. "Today I was called in for that meeting."

It was unfuckingbelievable! She had trusted the chaplain with her burden, and he had apparently breached his ethical responsibility and abused Susanne's trust! The platoon leader claimed they had learned about us on their own, but the timing, and leadership's history of brazen lies, defied that explanation. I was broken and couldn't think of anything to say other than a pathetic "sorry" before we hung up.

Inside, the cameraman was ready for the interview. The correspondent picked up on my mood, so I explained the situation. She was as shocked as I and thought the story had great news value. I begged her off. I didn't want to create any more problems for Susanne than I already had.

After the interview, the correspondent delivered a folder containing my last will, written at my request by a Norwegian lawyer. If we went into Mosul, my chance of dying was relatively high. I wanted Susanne to inherit my apartment, hoping that might help her handle my death better. I signed the document with Eivind and Knut as witnesses.

Hirani, the correspondent and I would leave for the front the next day, but first we had Hirani's birthday to celebrate with Eivind and Knut. We took a cab to Ankawa and found a place that served alcohol. The atmosphere was somber; signing my will had been a bleak reminder of what might await Hirani and me in the upcoming offensive.

I reflected on Susanne's situation, and the more I thought, the angrier I got. I recalled a colleague at Rena who had continued working wearing an electronic ankle monitor after being sentenced to house arrest for reckless driving. A soldier in Dilshad's company had been caught brewing moonshine in the military garage and been reported to the police after trying to stab a conscript soldier. Not only had he stayed on, but he later received non-commissioned officer training. What had Susanne done to risk ejection from the Armed Forces? She had fallen in love with me.

I asked an acquaintance at Camp Rena to pass a message to the FSA, which was responsible for security clearances. I named the NRK personnel with me in Erbil and threatened to create a shitstorm unlike anything they had seen if Susanne lost her clearance.

I checked back with Susanne but didn't tell of her my plan if she were thrown out. She said an NCO officer in her unit had told two conscripts about us and the news had spread.

"Everyone in the squadron knows we're a couple," she said. "Soon the entire camp will know. People are already commenting and questioning me." I could hear her discouragement, which was entirely understandable. Leadership's handling of her personal situation was unprofessional at the very least.

"On the positive side, I no longer have to worry about people hitting on you," I joked. She groaned, and I hoped she smiled a bit at my bad humor.

Hirani and I returned to his aunt's house with Eivind and Knut for a couple hours' sleep. The next day we traveled to our front line with the NRK team to get footage from the field. We passed convoy upon convoy of Iraqi army vehicles headed for the Kurdish front. In Tel Skuf, the entire Iraqi brigade was in place. The long-awaited and decisive battle for Mosul was just around the corner.

20 FIRST WAVE

Failing health had forced the general to leave the front for several weeks. He was back in Baqofah, but the stress of leading the unit without official support had taken its toll and we worried.

I didn't know why our unit hadn't been paid or why we had so little official support. The general was enormously popular, almost a people's hero, and our unit had notably fought in several major battles since the outbreak of war two years earlier. It seemed almost as if the Kurdish leaders distanced themselves because of the general's past, although some had used his services as a hitman. It was quite ironic.

We would work closely with Iraqi forces during the coming operation, so the general invited a group of Iraqi officers and soldiers to dinner. We set up tables and chairs outside, and big plates of rice, boiled lamb, fried chicken, bread and vegetables were brought in from Duhok. For once we filled our stomachs with something other than rice; our pack of a dozen dogs feasted on the remains.

The Iraqis seemed decent, not the bloodthirsty Shiite war criminals they were portrayed as, but the offensive hadn't begun. How they would treat Mosul's Sunni population remained to be seen. After dinner, the general called a meeting of the Quick Reaction Force in the neighboring house.

"We'll probably get information about the offensive and who's participating," I said to James and Louis, who had also been invited. We sat on a couch with cups of tea and talked until the general entered. In unison, the group rose in silence until he sat.

The general confirmed rumors that the offensive would start on October 20, four days away. Our unit would, as expected, participate. We would attack in two waves. The general would lead the first, with around twenty Quick Reaction Force soldiers and infantry on the front line. The rest would form the second wave. The names of those in the first wave would be announced sometime that night; the general expected everyone to respect his choices. Soldiers in the first wave would naturally face the greatest risk but fighting alongside the general was a great honor. Placement in the second wave would be a disappointment for many.

I lingered after the meeting until only the general and Deldar remained. I had to be part of the first wave. I had waited for this battle for more than a year and a half and had earned my spot among the first to attack. It could be hours or even days before the second wave was activated, and even then, they might miss out on the real action. I had always addressed the general respectfully and from a place of deference, but this time I couldn't stand idly by.

"General, I expect I'm in the first wave?" I asked, trying not to plead. He hesitated, as if he hadn't yet decided, then nodded slowly.

"You're in." I smiled from ear to ear and hugged him. I loved this man!

That night, the first wave list was posted in the living room. Many in my unit were disappointed, including Hirani, who had been assigned the second wave. I was surprised; I had assumed he would be with me. The general knew we had been inseparable since he joined our unit.

"Mike, either I fight with you, or not at all," Hirani said. He recalled his phone call to me a couple months earlier when we were both home on leave. He had said he couldn't keep fighting at the front; that the strain on his family was too great. I understood him well. My own parents had been distraught by media coverage of the attack on Tel Skuf in May and other skirmishes in which I'd been involved. Hirani's family must be equally devastated knowing what their young, relatively untrained son was really doing.

"You have done your duty. Stay in Sweden with a good conscience," I said. "Find a job and start a new life." Hirani was the one in my unit I trusted the most, the one with whom I had the most in common. He was my true brother in arms and I would miss him terribly.

A week later Hirani changed his mind.

"I can't let you go to Mosul alone," he said. "I will go back to Baqofah with you, but this must be our last battle. After Mosul we both return home for good."

By returning to the front, Hirani was sacrificing his safety and his family's peace of mind. Fighting in wave one without him felt wrong. We pled our case to Deldar, one of the general's most trusted officers. He promised to do what he could to get Hirani moved to the first wave. We couldn't expect too much.

"The general is probably afraid of losing both of you," he said.

James and Louis had been assigned to the second wave and were very happy to participate in the offensive at all. All their hard work throughout the summer was finally paying off.

Later that night, Deldar returned with good news. Hirani could join the first wave. James, Louis, Hirani and I immediately began to prepare. It was hard to predict how long we would be gone, or under what conditions we would be living. We knew absolutely nothing about the operation other than the start date and the initial goal of taking the neighboring town of Batnaya.

"Pack smart, Hirani. Bring only the essentials," I advised. "Prioritize extra ammunition, medical supplies and gun maintenance equipment. And bring a warm jacket; we'll probably sleep under open skies. Bring a French field ration too." We were allowed a single backpack each and couldn't afford such luxuries as sleeping bags, sleeping pads or extra clothes. Then we waited. James and Louis pestered us constantly for updates.

"We don't know shit, Buddy," I said as Louis plied me with a can of Wild Tiger. "It's always like this. They tell us nothing.

"When the operation starts, just follow the flow and try to stay alive." The windows shook as another bomb dropped over Batnaya.

"Holy fuck, that was a big one!" James said, laughing. "The way the Coalition is bombing now, there won't be anyone left alive when we arrive."

"Don't be so sure," Louis said. "The intelligence guys I talk to in the States say Daesh has dug a bunch of tunnels under Batnaya, Tel Keppe and Mosul."

The tunnels worried me. ISIS used boring machines and slaves to dig intricate networks under the cities and towns they controlled. The good guys entered the cities without encountering resistance, only to be surrounded and destroyed once inside. Despite that and other risks, I looked forward to starting the operation after nearly two years on the front line. I was getting tired, physically and mentally. I wanted to achieve my goal and go home to Norway, hopefully alive.

The evening before the offensive began, Hirani and I made our final preparations in the bedroom, then turned off the lights and went to bed, hoping for a few hours' sleep. Hirani played classical music softly on his phone, a welcome change from his usual rap. I closed my eyes and listened to the symphony. In the distance I could hear mortar grenades hitting our front line. Daesh was still alive in Batnaya. Soon I would stand face to face with them. I was completely calm and relaxed. I was just about asleep when the order came.

"Get up, get ready. We are leaving," Karwan barked as he switched on the lights. I looked at my watch, it was barely past midnight.

"Come on, Hirani," I urged, and forced myself out of bed. "We can rest when we're dead!" Outside the streets were bustling. Vehicles and squad weapons were readied, and soldiers loaded backpacks and equipment into pickup trucks. James and Louis arrived with some of the Assyrians.

"Where do you want us?" James asked. Our second in command appeared.

"They can't join us. New orders, sorry," he told one of the Assyrians, who translated into English. I didn't understand. The general had promised them a spot in the second wave. What had changed his mind? James and Louis were equally surprised. The general had already left, so we asked our second in command.

"Sorry, all I know is Wahed said that they can't join us after all." I was shocked and embarrassed.

I later learned the general had met with the president's son, Mansour Barzani, who had overall responsibility for the Kurdish forces in the coming offensive. Barzani had forbidden all Western volunteers from participating in the offensive under any circumstances. Wahed was taking a great risk allowing Hirani and me to fight. It would have sealed his fate had he allowed Western-looking Louis and James to go. Hirani and I looked at each other across the truck bed as we headed out of Baqofah. It was hard leaving James and Louis behind. They must be heartbroken. I would have been.

We paralleled the front line along a dirt road eastward for half an hour to the rendezvous point, where we joined other large local units and American special forces with modern armored vehicles for the advance to Batnaya.

During such a military operation back home, every soldier would be informed about the plan in detail. Everyone would understand exactly what was going to happen and their role in it. Here, only top leadership were privy to the plan. All we knew was that we would attack Batnaya from the east. I had gotten used to being left in the dark.

At dawn, several wheel loaders dug through the berm at the front line and filled in the trench on the other side so we could drive into no man's land. Our unit was among the first to advance. Oh, what a magical moment it was crossing the front line and driving into ISIS territory! It was finally our turn to be on the offensive. Now we were the hunters.

An armored demining vehicle led the convoy. Our unit and our neighboring unit followed in unarmored pickup trucks and SUVs. The other local units, the Americans and more civilian wheel loaders brought up the rear. The road to Batnaya was long and we stopped frequently while deminers neutralized buried roadside bombs. Even a small bomb could easily destroy any of our vehicles and everyone in it. I was grateful for the deminers, but the constant delays were frustrating. I sat in the passenger seat and impatiently tapped my fingers against the dashboard.

"Suicide vehicle!" a voice shouted. I looked around the relatively flat, open landscape to a small hill on our left. The vehicle had to be behind it. I jumped out of the cab. Hirani jumped out of the bed. A neighboring unit's pickup with a mounted wire-guided anti-tank missile drove forward into a defensive position. Armed only with rifles, there was little Hirani and I could do. I looked in vain for a ditch or a mound where we could take cover. The surrounding area was completely flat. All we could do was wait and hope for the best.

An armored vehicle appeared from behind the hill, less than 250 yards away. The pickup fired its missile, which hit the ground and ricocheted above the oncoming vehicle.

"Fuck, are you kidding me? He missed!" Hirani shouted. Panic seized some of our ranks while others prepared to fire rockets and grenades.

"Don't shoot, it's our own!" someone yelled. I couldn't believe it. It was a Peshmerga vehicle from another unit. It had been pure luck that our missile had been badly off target.

Our driver had disappeared, so Hirani and I got into another pickup and continued advancing. This truck had improvised armor of a steel frame, corrugated steel sheets and sandbags. Necessity is the mother of invention, it is said. Six of us were packed like sardines into the bed; comfort was impossible with boxes of ammunition and weapons strewn everywhere. As we approached Batnaya the sky was black with smoke. ISIS was burning oil again.

We passed a small village on the plains and enemy fire erupted. So, they intended to resist; that was good. I peered over the sandbags to pinpoint the fire's origin in the village several hundred yards away. Adrenaline slowly spread through my body, but I was calm.

It was hard to make reliable observations as we bumped along the rutted dirt road. Enemy machine guns rang out intensely. A bullet hit our windshield and the driver hit the gas. The vehicle behind us was also hit. Daesh was targeting our part of the convoy. We drove at full speed until we reached a fitting place and could return fire.

"Get out, get out!" our driver shouted. I found cover behind the hood and looked through my scope. The village was small, but I couldn't identify the gunfire's source. There couldn't be many enemy in there, maybe a handful tasked with delaying our advance. Our men started shooting towards the buildings with heavy and light machine guns as other units and the Americans passed us.

"I can't see anything, can you?" I shouted to Hirani, who stood behind the pickup.

"Yes, there's a car coming. Fuck, it's a suicide vehicle!" he replied. I couldn't see anything from where I stood.

"Are you sure?" I shouted.

"Yes. It has to be. It has steel plates welded on it."

Others had seen the vehicle and panic was spreading. Some ran away, others jumped into cars and drove off and others stood around perplexed. If anything could scare Peshmerga soldiers, it was those fucking suicide vehicles.

"Mike, come, we're leaving," Hirani said as he headed for a pickup.

"Fuck no," I said firmly. I had no plan. All I knew was that I wouldn't flee.

Historically, many battles have been won not by killing the opponent, but by spreading fear and panic among them. A few fleeing soldiers was usually enough to start a stampede within the ranks. The defense would collapse, and the enemy would slaughter the remaining soldiers with ease.

I would not succumb, even though I also felt fear. Hirani looked at me dejectedly, as if to say, "Do you always have to play the hero?" A second later he threw his rifle on the truck's bed, grabbed an RPG-7 grenade launcher and ran towards the village.

"Yes, Hirani, run!" I shouted.

I took off after him, caught up, placed my left hand on his right shoulder and pushed him forward, so he'd know he wasn't alone and wouldn't waver. The guys shouted for us to come back, but we were deaf to their entreaties. We were meeting the threat face to face. I had never been more impressed by Hirani, who was now willing to sacrifice his own life for his fellow soldiers. I was infinitely proud of my brother in arms and the courage he displayed. I wouldn't let him die alone.

As we ran, the suicide vehicle abruptly turned and drove back to the village, where it retreated behind some buildings. Hirani and I were now totally exposed in the middle of the flat plain outside the village. We needed a new plan.

The pickup with the wire-guided anti-tank missile got into position behind us. After its failure earlier in the day, I didn't have much confidence it could hit the suicide vehicle, should it return.

I had an idea. Hirani and I sprinted toward the front of the convoy until we found the American special forces soldiers.

"Suicide vehicle... in the village... over there," was all I managed to choke out.

"Oh shit," An American shouted. "Guys, there's a suicide vehicle in the village behind us!" The Americans manned four armored vehicles with all kinds of weapon systems on board, including the high-tech Javelin missile, which could easily take out the suicide vehicle.

A big, muscular soldier wearing a helmet, shades and a moustache that covered his entire mouth, stepped from his vehicle. He held a 60mm mortar tube and appeared completely calm in the face of the news I had just served.

"We're in a firefight with snipers in that farm," he said as his top cover opened fire against buildings half a mile away. "But we have an AC-130 in the area. We'll send the coordinates and ask it to take out the suicide vehicle." The AC-130 is a heavily armed close air support gunship based on the C-130 Hercules transport used by the Norwegian armed forces. Only a dozen of this aircraft exists; it has a legendary reputation among soldiers worldwide.

"This is going to be good," I thought as the Americans blasted the farm with mortar grenades.

Hirani and I ran down the line of vehicles warning the others to avoid the village. Not long after, I thought I heard the dull roar of an engine above through the shooting around us. A powerful explosion erupted from the village followed by billowing smoke and debris. The suicide vehicle had met its maker and I hadn't even seen the aircraft. I understood why the AC-130 had such a reputation.

We continued advancing towards Batnaya under sporadic fire from nearby settlements and buildings. I was in my element. In the afternoon, a supply truck delivered food, and our spirits rose again. We found cover to eat behind the vehicle and sat with our Styrofoam boxes of rice, chicken, cucumber and tomato. I plucked out the tomato and took a big bite, juice flying. I hadn't eaten since the previous evening; I grinned with pleasure at the delicious meal and the fighting so far. Hirani looked at me and shook his head, smiling.

"Look at him," he said to the guys around us. "Normally he's the world's nicest and calmest guy, but as soon as there's shooting, he becomes a wild animal." The others nodded.

"Until Mike showed up last year, I never thought I'd meet someone who loved fighting more than Wahed," Karwan added. I said nothing. They were right. I was normally calm and reserved, but during battle, a side of me that few in Norway had seen, awoke.

The closer we got to Batnaya, the more fire we received. We stopped a few hundred yards from town where our wheel loaders were digging berms for cover. The courageous drivers, civilians who suddenly found themselves at the forefront of the battle, were completely exposed as bullets hit their vehicles. It was hard not to be impressed.

The berm quickly rose to form a large circle around us. It looked like an outpost deep inside enemy territory. US and Iraqi forces pulled into the enclosure with us. Bullets whizzed past our heads from several directions and we returned fire with everything we had. The Americans called in airstrike after airstrike. The Iraqis returned enemy fire with 120mm mortars. The town turned to gravel before our eyes. As evening approached I realized we wouldn't take Batnaya that day.

"We'll probably stay here for a few days, until the airstrikes have done their work," Deldar said. "Then we'll move in."

Incoming fire decreased as daylight disappeared. The other units had guard duty the first night, so we decided to get some sleep. I surveyed our provisional outpost. All the good sleeping spots on our vehicles were taken. I put on my down jacket and woolen hat and covered my face with a scarf. With my backpack as a pillow and my rifle next to me, I lay down on the cold, dusty ground and closed my eyes. Although I hadn't gotten any rest the previous night, sleep eluded me. Just as I drifted off, the chill air or a guard shooting imagined enemies would jolt me awake. I listened until the guards realized there was nobody out there, then closed my eyes again.

Sometime later, shooting commenced in earnest and bullets whizzed above my head from outside the berm. I grabbed my rifle and ran to the outpost's south side. The shooting intensified. I was met by a sea of tracers in both directions and loud reports from weapons on all sides. We were under attack.

"They're coming from Tel Keppe!" Nahman shouted as he readied his machine gun.

"They have suicide vehicles too," Hirani added. "We saw two turn their headlights on for a second."

I peered into the darkness. Enemy muzzle flash looked like glittering stars on the horizon; it was beautiful.

A long burst of tracer bullets flew right above my head. Had I been upright, I would have caught the entire burst. I adjusted my scope and started picking out potential targets. American special forces ran toward us and established themselves on the berm. With their night vision and thermal scopes, they could locate the enemy with ease.

"There's a whole bunch of them, at least twenty or thirty on foot and three potential suicide vehicles!" the American beside me shouted. ISIS was serious this time.

One American had a .50 caliber sniper rifle, which was powerful enough to stop a large truck.

"I'm engaging the nearest vehicle," he said and pulled the trigger. Dust swirled up as the bullet left the weapon with a deafening bang. Sparks shot through the dark as the armor-piercing round hit the vehicle.

"Hit!" he shouted.

"It's not stopping. Ready a Javelin!" another American shouted.

The vehicle must have welded steel plates so thick not even a .50 caliber round could penetrate. The Americans picked up and loaded the Javelin, comprised of a targeting component and tube containing the missile itself. Some Telemark Battalion platoons possessed this high-tech weapon system, but I had never seen it fired. The Javelin operator locked onto the target as I eagerly watched from my front row seat.

"Firing!" he shouted.

A flame kicked out of the tube's rear and the missile, tube and firing component flew five yards to the opposite side of the berm, followed by silence.

"Fuck, the lid was still on!" the American cursed.

"What lid?" another asked.

"The one on the Javelin," the first replied. Something had gone wrong, but I wasn't sure what. They readied a new missile in record time.

"Firing!" the operator shouted again. This attempt met with success and cheers from everyone. The missile rose majestically into the air and found its target from above. An explosion broke the night to more cheers.

"Two vehicles remaining," I thought, until an American pointed to the first vehicle, still creeping toward us. How was it possible? From the little I knew of the Javelin's precision, it was nearly impossible to miss a slow-moving target.

"We have an AC-130 on the way!" an American shouted. Shielded by darkness, the suicide vehicles continued toward us.

With their advanced optics and large caliber bullets, the Americans could keep engaging them. Sparks against the vehicles confirmed the hits, but they had little effect. Death moved unwaveringly closer.

"That aircraft must get here soon," I thought. The number of tracers above us had gradually increased and the situation was not looking good.

Four or five hundred yards away, the first suicide vehicle erupted in flame and debris as an aircraft passed above us. The aircraft took out the other two in rapid succession before targeting the ISIS fighters on foot with its 40mm cannon. Burst after burst rained down on the jihadists, just a few hundred yards away. The large projectiles formed small, delicate sparkles as they exploded and wiped out the enemy in front of our eyes. The plane's thermal optics made it impossible for ISIS to hide. For more than fifteen minutes, the plane circled above us and killed mercilessly.

Just as we thought it was over, we heard the whistle of an incoming missile and barely managed to get down before an enormous explosion rocked the outpost's north side.

"What the fuck was that?" the Americans asked, almost in unison. One picked up the radio and quickly received an answer. An undetected suicide vehicle had snuck up on us from the north. A fighter jet had spotted it and saved our skins. I couldn't imagine the carnage had the

Americans not been with us that night.

21 THE LIBERATION OF BATNAYA

The next morning, we awoke to incoming mortar grenades hitting around the outpost.

"120mm. They're coming from Tel Keppe," a soldier from the neighboring unit said.

Tel Keppe was the last town between us and Mosul. It had been a Christian town of more than 40,000 inhabitants when ISIS had taken Mosul two years earlier. With the residents of Batnaya, Tel Skuf and the surrounding areas, the non-Muslim population had fled during a single night, barely escaping the Islamists and a grisly fate.

The distance to Tel Keppe was too great for us to retaliate with our weapons, so the Americans readied their 81mm mortars on the outpost's south side, while the Iraqis resumed bombing Batnaya with 120mm mortars from the north side.

An American prepared a vehicle-mounted automatic 40mm grenade launcher. As he knocked the lid down and cocked the weapon, he shouted "Say hello to my little friend," in a Cuban accent. I smiled at the reference to Al Pacino's legendary line from the movie "Scarface," as he fired his 40mm grenade launcher.

The American's grenade launcher spit out grenade after grenade as enemy mortars rained down outside our outpost. Just a single grenade hit inside would cause heavy losses. The Americans returned fire with their mortars, and eventually things calmed down.

Some of the guys gathered around our cars and listened to the news on the radio.

"Has something happened?" I asked Hirani.

"Daesh is attacking Kirkuk. There's a full-blown war there now."

Kirkuk was one of the Kurdish Region's largest and most important cities due to its strategic location and the area's large oil deposits. ISIS had smuggled more than one hundred fighters into the city under the cover of darkness. The next morning, they mounted a two-day battle that killed large numbers of security forces and civilians, including a good friend of Hirani's. He took it hard.

"His name was Muhammad. We served together in my old unit in Kirkuk. May he rest in peace," Hirani said.

ISIS' attack on Kirkuk was an obvious attempt to divert media attention from the Mosul offensive. The terrorists knew they were doomed to lose their self-proclaimed capital and wanted to show both the world and potential recruits they were still capable of executing offensive operations.

We spent five days at the outpost under constant indirect fire from Tel Keppe as we waited for the green light to advance into Batnaya. Several grenades and rockets hit so close that gravel and dirt rained down on us. Early on October 25, the order finally came. We were taking Batnaya.

The town had been obliterated during the last days, and I doubted we would encounter much resistance. Roadside bombs, booby-traps and tunnels hiding suicide bombers were our primary concern.

We left the outpost in the middle of the night. I threw my backpack in the trunk of our unit's only armored vehicle, a black Humvee, and climbed behind the wheel. The Humvee had been a reward from the government after the attack on Tel Skuf in May. Nahman positioned himself in the roof hatch as top cover with his machine gun, and a high-ranking security service officer sat in the passenger seat. I fired up the engine and joined the queue near the front of the convoy. For more than two years ISIS had controlled Batnaya. Today, their reign of terror would come to an end.

Once the Iraqis fired their final grenade on Batnaya we drove towards the town, a demining vehicle leading the charge. We stopped frequently to neutralize roadside bombs, or for soldiers to open fire on phantom ISIS fighters inside demolished buildings. We received no incoming fire. The few ISIS fighters we encountered lay rotting in the October sun, surrounded by buzzing flies. After driving through the town unchallenged, we declared Batnaya liberated.

I walked over to what had been ISIS' front line to look towards Baqofah. It was poignant to finally breathe in this view; to see what the enemy had seen for the last two years. I had waited for this moment for a long time, but it was a bit of a letdown. I had imagined the battle for Batnaya being harder, and the victory greater.

My disappointment didn't stop there. During the last days it had become clear that the Peshmerga wouldn't participate in the battle for Mosul itself. We would stop at Batnaya and the Iraqi forces would advance on Tel Keppe and Mosul alone. The order came from high up. It was hard for me to accept.

For more than two years I had dreamed of fighting in Mosul; of seeing the black ISIS flags torn from buildings and lit on fire; of witnessing the Caliphate crushed from the inside. Should the Kurds, who had suffered so much under the Islamists' ravages, be left out of the decisive battle because of political disagreements between Erbil and Bagdad? After all, Mosul had had a large Kurdish population before ISIS conquered the city. It was only fair that we participate. I held out some hope that the Iraqis would ask for our assistance when they experienced major losses in Tel Keppe and Mosul, but deep down I knew it was unlikely.

"We have one target left," the general announced. The village we had passed the first day was home to Mar Oraha, a Sixth Century monastery with great significance for the area's Christians. We set our course for the village, entering with the Americans without resistance.

Soldiers from the neighboring unit had brought a large wooden cross to replace the original one, removed by ISIS. They hefted the replacement up to the monastery's roof and as they raised it beside the Kurdish flag, wild cheering erupted, and the guys fired into the air to celebrate the victory. That my fellow soldiers, who were mostly Muslims, expressed such respect for another religion, filled me with pride.

While the others celebrated, I continued into the village alone on foot. There I found the wreck of the suicide vehicle that had abruptly retreated the first day of the offensive. It was loaded with large, undetonated explosive-filled cylinders, but the car was completely burned out.

A charred body lay face down in the dirt next to the open driver's door. This was the driver who, for reasons we would never know, had abandoned his attack. He was scrawny, most likely a young teenager, or even a child.

The thought of the boy's last hour gripped me. He must have been scared for his life, as he sat in the driver's seat. Was that why he had turned around? Had he been forced behind the wheel by the Islamists? Children and teenagers don't possess an innate desire to blow themselves up, no matter where in the world they come from. What might have happened if I hadn't notified the Americans of the vehicle. Would he still be alive? Flies buzzed hungrily around the burned body. Nothing could be done now. We were alive, and that was what mattered. I turned and returned to the others.

We spent the next week at the outpost with daily trips to Batnaya to search houses and the networks of tunnels we discovered. Jacques and the French special forces were back. They helped locate and map tunnels and remove the booby-traps ISIS had left behind. Several Peshmerga soldiers were killed disarming booby-traps; three were killed and four injured when a massive bomb blew up one of the tunnels while I watched. A French team had nearly succumbed to friendly fire when they emerged from a hidden tunnel and surprised some Peshmerga soldiers from behind.

"They thought we were Daesh and opened fire," the French leader told me, laughing. "Luckily, they missed."

As we began declaring the town safe, public authorities and religious leaders arrived, followed by a steady stream of reporters and cameramen. The cross on the old Batnaya church in Batnaya was to be restored, which the media would thoroughly document.

The general assigned me and several others to ensure the visitors' safety. For some time, I had hoped to see the church up close. It was visible from our front line and we had often spotted activity there. Perhaps ISIS strategists knew the Coalition wouldn't bomb it. But it had suffered great damage, most likely from Iraqi and Peshmerga mortar grenades.

"Look, that's probably our doing," the general said proudly pointing to a hole in the roof from an 82mm grenade.

The Islamists had completely destroyed the interior and all Christian symbols and artifacts had been removed or vandalized. How could ISIS justify these acts? If their God was as almighty as they claimed, would he really want a gang of bullies vandalizing in his name? Would their God accept the cruel acts his followers committed against other Muslims and those of different faiths? I doubted it.

As the visitors moved up the stairs to the roof, I noticed Noel, the Frenchman who had delivered my new pistol sight, busily taking pictures of the altar. I approached him and patted his shoulder.

"No way, Mike? How are you?" he asked, smiling. As before, he had a Glock pistol discreetly hidden under his shirt, but visible to the trained eye.

I told him my plan to go home in time for Christmas if we were barred from the battle for Tel Skuf and Mosul, and I offered to visit him in Erbil with Hirani, and volunteer for his aid organization before we left for good. It would be a nice way to end our time in Northern Iraq. If we couldn't take part in liberating Mosul, perhaps we could do something for the people who had fled because of the war. Noel seemed grateful for the offer and said he would ask his boss. I followed him to the roof where he got good photos of the bishop stepping the cross.

I hoped life here would return to normal soon, but it was unlikely. The town was completely ravaged, and the once large Christian population in Iraq, which had been subjected to Islamic persecution since the 2003 American invasion, was disappearing from the country completely.

The Assyrians from Dwekh Nawsha showed up at our outpost one day without James, Louis or the other Western volunteers. We had been shelled all day, but it had been quiet for about an hour when they arrived in a pickup truck. A coincidence? They had come to take promotional pictures of themselves outside Batnaya and were clearly nervous being in an area that, just a few days earlier, had belonged to ISIS. I secretly hoped ISIS would fire a few more grenades while the Assyrians were there, as close to the outpost as possible.

As the days passed, I slowly accepted that Batnaya was the nearest I would get to Mosul. Iraqi forces were about to seize Tel Keppe. As expected, they suffered heavy losses daily. Outside Batnaya I befriended a Kurdish ambulance driver and his Iraqi partner who had their hands full transporting injured and dead Iraqi soldiers from Tel Keppe to Duhok. In a final, desperate attempt to get closer to Mosul, I offered to volunteer on the ambulance. I was willing to get rid of my uniform and rifle, if that was what it took. The driver refused my help.

"Tel Keppe is a bloodbath. We lose medics every day and I don't want your life on my conscience." With that I realized it was over. I could do nothing more under the current conditions. It was time to go home.

Hirani and I returned to Baqofah and prepared for the trip home. We were almost alone in the village. James, Louis, and the other Western volunteers had gone to Erbil, and we decided to do the same.

"We could spend a couple of weeks in Erbil and Sulaymaniyah and say goodbye to everyone," I suggested. "This might be the last time we see Kurdistan."

We said our farewells to the few guys left in Baqofah and gave them the clothes and equipment we no longer needed. It was sad to see how grateful they were for used boots, gloves and other gear most soldiers took for granted.

We wished them good luck then Deldar drove us to the weapons market in Duhok. With his help I sold my weapon and remaining ammunition. As expected I took a couple thousand dollars' loss, but I still had enough to take Susanne on a vacation once I got home and I was satisfied with the transaction. The weapons had done their job.

Finally, we returned to the house to say goodbye to the general. I thanked him for letting us fight by his side and gave him my scope as a parting gift. The scope on his M4 rifle was old and had taken a beating; he greatly appreciated the gesture.

"It's been an honor having you here. I wish I had something to give you, but you know how the situation is," he said, clearly embarrassed.

"Neither of us came here for money," I assured him. "We came to do our duty, and you can't put a price on the battles we saw with you." He was touched and seemed genuinely sad we were leaving.

"Tell the world what you experienced here," he asked. "Tell them back home how we fought, and what we sacrificed."

Hirani and I left the house while Deldar stayed with the general for a moment.

"Okay, let's go," Deldar said with a sigh when he emerged. "I'll drive you to the taxi central, and from there you can get to Erbil on your own.

"Wahed started crying after you two left," he said after a few moments. "He's very sad you're leaving."

I felt for the general. He was a man of war. To fight was what he did best. He also loved the enormous popularity that resulted from his battle against the Islamists. Like most humans, he enjoyed feeling important and useful. Would the people need him now that the fight was over?

Deldar had been a good friend and very helpful throughout my time at the front and he was one of the few reliable Quick Reaction Force officers left. As a thank you I gave him my reserve scope and a couple of hand grenades.

"Take good care of Wahed," I said. "He needs all the support he can get from you guys now." We said goodbye and caught a cab to Erbil.

We would stay at Hirani's aunt's house for a week, then travel to Sulaymaniyah and, finally, home to Scandinavia. His aunt was away, so we had the house to ourselves. We spent time with friends we had gotten to know during our stay in the country; journalists, aid workers and other Western volunteers, including James and Louis, who were also going home. They were understandably bitter over having been left out of the offensive, especially James. He tried hiding it, but it was easy to see he was disheartened.

"We invested so much time and money, we risked our lives at the front line only to be eliminated from the offensive at the last minute," he said. "It sucks, but what can you do?" They deserved better after all they had done for us.

We also met with Noel. He introduced us to his boss, who turned out to be a huge fan of both Hirani and me; Hirani had also achieved social media fame during his time with me.

Noel's boss offered to hire us as a part of the French aid workers' security force. We politely declined but offered to volunteer during our stay in Erbil. The French organization provided aid to Christian and Yazidi refugees and although Hirani was a faithful Muslim and I came from a Muslim family, we both wanted to lend a helping hand.

We visited a refugee camp in Ankawa where we handed out toys, entertained children and played chess with the elders. The conditions were relatively good compared to those in the large tent camps we had seen on the plains, but I still felt sorry for them. As a religious minority in an increasingly divided Iraq, Christians and Yazidis had an uncertain future.

Our last evening in Erbil, Hirani and I visited a market he knew, going from vendor to vendor tasting everything they had to offer: lamb livers, chicken hearts, sheep testicles grilled on spears, pancakes, freshly pressed juice and tea. Living in poverty, misery and near starvation had put things in perspective. From then on, I would appreciate the little things in life in a totally different way.

On our way to Sulaymaniyah the next day we visited Alex. His tactical training center outside Erbil was nearing completion and we had fun shooting at one of the ranges with rifles and pistols before an assistant put meat on the grill for our meal. Alex and the elite force he had trained had fought in the October 21 attack on Kirkuk, and we enjoyed watching the footage from his helmet camera during dinner.

"Look, Daesh barricaded themselves inside this elementary school," he enthusiastically narrated. "We went from room to room, and I was always the first one in!" Gunshots popped from his laptop.

Again, he offered me a job at the training center and his company, AP TAC.

"What are you going to do in Norway, Mike? Work nine to five in an office?" he asked. "That life isn't for people like us. You know that. Here there will always be war, even after Daesh is destroyed, and there will always be a need for us."

I respected Alex and I knew he had a point. We had a lot in common; we both had professional military backgrounds and strong warrior mentalities, skills not all soldiers possessed. We were battle-tested and had developed a taste for war. That's not something easily left behind. Could I adapt to civilian life back home after my experiences at the front? Or would the longing for adrenaline and fear, the sound of grenades and the smell of gunpowder be too great? I didn't know. But I had to at least give the normal life a try. I owed it to Susanne and my family.

EPILOGUE

Norway, August 5, 2018

Two months after my return to Norway, I received news that the general had suffered a stroke and died peacefully in his own bed. They called it natural causes, but I knew better. For more than two years Wahed had led our unit with almost no outside support. He had lost beloved family members, friends and his own men in the war against ISIS. He had spent countless sleepless nights at the front, survived on a terrible diet, smoked thousands of cigarettes and accepted responsibilities few could even imagine. He wasn't killed by enemy bullets, but he was a victim of the war.

Hirani went home to Sweden and tried his best to adapt to civilian life. He developed symptoms of PTSD, which was perhaps inevitable. He had been thrown into a brutal war at eighteen, without the previous military experience or necessary mental preparations of a professional soldier. With few options available at home, Hirani returned to the Middle East this summer. As I write, he's completing training with the YPG and will soon be shipped to a front to fight once again. We talk almost every day. I consider Hirani one of my closest friends.

Louis joined the United States Marine Corps as an infantry reservist and studies on the side. The Brits James, Jim, and Tim all live in the UK as civilians, as do Eivind and Knut here in Norway. Karl Håkon on the other hand, returned to the Middle East after a few months home and joined the PKK. He was recently injured fighting in Syria and lost sight in one eye.

Susanne was allowed to continue her conscription. Whether it was my threats, or because she never was in any real danger of losing her security clearance is hard to say. The controversy felt highly unnecessary and did nothing to improve my relationship with the armed forces. She now studies and I work at an office in Oslo where none of my colleagues know about my past. Susanne and I recently I bought a new house in a small village outside the city, close to the fjord. We're moving in with our one-year-old dog Léon as I write, and I'm looking forward to living the quiet life with the woman I love.

On July,10 2017, the Iraqi prime minister declared Mosul liberated after nearly nine months of bloody urban combat. The city was completely destroyed and, as expected, Iraqi forces suffered heavy losses. The Islamists used every dirty trick in the book to make the Iraqi victory as costly as possible including human shields, car bombs, suicide bombers hidden among fleeing civilians and chemical attacks.

The Coalition-supported mainly Shiite Iraqi army retaliated by committing large-scale war crimes against both suspected and confirmed ISIS members and Mosul's civilian Sunni population. Their crimes included public executions, torture, rape and kidnapping.

The battle for Mosul was a display of the worst, most brutal and barbaric of human nature. And it is far from over. Sunni Muslims will eventually seek revenge and the cycle of violence will continue as it has for centuries.

For me, the war against ISIS confirmed what I have known for a long time. That we live in a world where the strongest will rule when there's anarchy, that the most effective way to reach ones' goals is through violence, that nature is cruel, and that there is no happy ending. This may sound bleak, but this realization has made me capable of appreciating what I have at home in Norway. I live in a democratic society with law and order, freedom of speech and religious and gender equality. I'm surrounded by luxury every day, although many around me aren't even aware of it.

I have been very lucky. I returned home without physical or emotional damage and that isn't something I take for granted. I have learned to appreciate life and what I have in a totally new way. For better or worse, my fight against the Caliphate was two years I will never regret.

Mike Peshmerganor

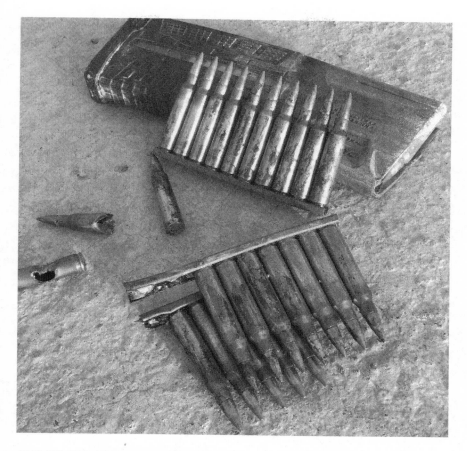

AMMUNITION TAKEN FROM KILLED ISIS FIGHTERS AFTER THE
BATTLE OF TEL SKUF. AFTER I WASHED AWAY THE BLOOD,
MOST OF IT WAS AS GOOD AS NEW.

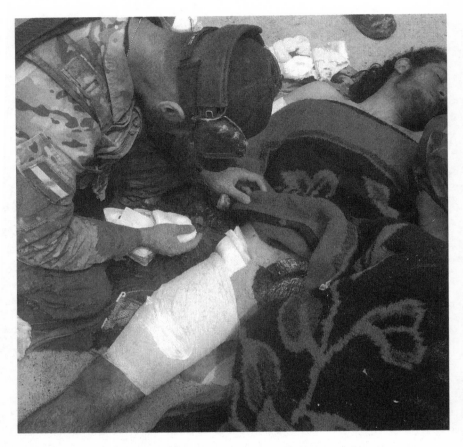

ME TREATING CAPTURED ISIS FIGHTER ABU ESHAQ, OUTSIDE
THE TEL SKUF FIELD HOSPITAL. NOTICE THE SMALL PIECE OF
FLESH AND THE BLOOD TRAIL ON MY HEARING PROTECTION,
REMAINS OF A SUICIDE BOMBER I WAS UNAWARE OF.

**DELDAR DURING THE ADVANCE TOWARDS BATNAYA, WITH
OUR GUYS IN THE BACKGROUND.**

TWO LOCAL SOLDIERS AND ME AFTER THE BATTLE AT THE ASKI MOSUL FRONT.

BREAKFAST WITH LOUIS AND TWO OF THE GUYS AFTER A LONG NIGHT AT THE FRONT LINE; FLATBREAD SPRINKLED WITH WATER, YOGURT AND TEA MADE UP THE MENU.

AIRPORT SECURITY CONFISCATING MORE THAN $3,000 IN EQUIPMENT IN ERBIL.

THE QUICK REACTION FORCE IN BAQOFAH.

THE CRATER CREATED BY THE 120MM MORTAR GRENADE THAT STRUCK JUST OVER 50 YARDS AWAY FROM AYHAN AND ME. THE SOFT GROUND ABSORBED MOST OF THE GRENADE AND SHRAPNEL, SAVING OUR LIVES.

THE TRENCH THAT SEPARATED US FROM ISIS, WITH NO MAN'S LAND AND THE CALIPHATE ON THE OTHER SIDE.

MY HEARING PROTECTION WITH A SUICIDE BOMBER'S REMAINS ON IT.

WITH IRAQI SOLDIERS OUTSIDE BATNAYA, WHICH HAD JUST BEEN BOMBED BY COALITION WARPLANES.

ONE OF THE PRISONERS WE TOOK DURING THE LIBERATION OF SINJAR.

BRITISH JAMES AND TIM IN DUHOK WITH THE HEATERS THEY BOUGHT FOR US.

HIRANI AND ME DURING THE BATTLE OF TEL SKUF, WITH ISIS-CONTROLLED BATNAYA IN THE BACKGROUND.

PESHMERGA SOLDIERS WITH THE CORPSES OF TWO ISIS FIGHTERS. THE OFFICER IN THE MIDDLE IS WEARING A NORWEGIAN UNIFORM, PROBABLY A CHINESE COPY BOUGHT CHEAPLY OVER THE INTERNET.

AT THE FRONT WITH NORWEGIAN MAX-HENDRIK AND NICK, FROM THE AID ORGANIZATION GSMSG.

WESTERN VOLUNTEERS FROM DWEKH NAWSHA AND ME.

ONE OF THE ISIS FIGHTERS WE KILLED ON MAY 4, 2016.

SPOILS OF WAR AFTER SINJAR; AN ISIS FLAG AND SEVERAL SWEDISH-MADE ROCKET LAUNCHERS.

HIRANI, THE GENERAL AND ME ON THE FRONT LINE.

THE ADVANCE ON BATNAYA, OCTOBER 20, 2016.

NAHMAN AND HIS PKM MACHINE GUN.

ON OUR WAY TOWARDS ISIS-CONTROLLED BATNAYA.

MY BED IN THE ASSYRIAN VILLAGE OF BAQOFAH.

THE SCANDINAVIAN GROUP, FROM LEFT: KNUT, JESPER, BRITISH MARK WITH KARL HÅKON IN FRONT.

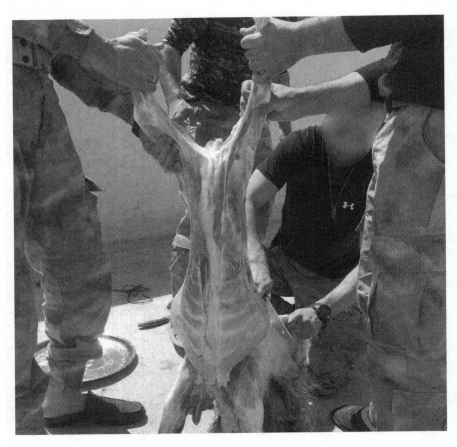

SLAUGHTERING A GOAT THE HALAL WAY IN BAQOFAH.

HIRANI AND ME DURING THE MOSUL OFFENSIVE.

THE TEDDY BEAR I FOUND FOR SUSANNE AFTER THE BATTLE OF TEL SKUF.

BACK IN SINJAR AFTER THE LIBERATION; LOOKING FOR A HIDDEN WEAPON CACHE WE RECEIVED A TIP ABOUT.

THE GENERAL GIVING ORDERS DURING THE LIBERATION OF BATNAYA.

THE GENERAL WITH AN EXECUTED ISIS FIGHTER DURING THE FIGHTING IN TEL SKUF.

**THE GENERAL GETTING STITCHES WITHOUT ANESTHESIA
AFTER BEING HIT BY SHRAPNEL FROM A MORTAR GRENADE.**